Contents

"The day we stop exploring is the day we commit ourselves to live in a stagnant world, devoid of curiosity and wonder."

— Neil deGrasse Tyson

1. A New Vision: The Human and Machine Confluence

In the age of exponential technological advancement, the boundaries between what is considered human and what is perceived as machine are becoming increasingly blurred. The heart of this transformation lies in the field of cybernetic enhancements—a fascinating arena where biology meets technology, offering the potential to revolutionize the human condition. Rather than a distant science fiction narrative, these developments are becoming an integral part of our society, touching lives in ways previously unimagined.

This book, "Transhuman Transformations: An Exploration of Cybernetic Enhancements," seeks to take you on a comprehensive journey through the intricacies of this burgeoning field. It explores the motivations driving these developments, the technologies making them possible, and the profound implications they hold for our future. You'll journey with us from the philosophical underpinnings and ethical considerations to the pragmatic impacts and the visionary imaginations that fuel this exciting intersection of humanity and technology.

Whether you're a skeptic or an enthusiast, this exploration aims to not only inform but also inspire, inviting you to reflect on what it truly means to be human in the age of machines. Welcome to this pivotal moment in human history, where we ask not just "Can we?" but "Should we?" embark on this transformative path together.

2. The Origins of Cybernetic Dreams

2.1. The Human Desire for Enhancement

From the earliest records of human civilization, the desire for enhancement has been a persistent thread woven into our cultural fabric. Ancient myths and legends tell tales of heroes who possess extraordinary abilities, suggesting an ingrained yearning to transcend the limits of the human experience. Stories of gods and demigods, with powers that defy the laws of nature, speak to an innate human desire to reach beyond our mortal confines. This fascination with enhancement has persisted through history, manifesting in various forms, from early herbal remedies and alchemy to contemporary advancements in technology and biotechnology.

In the ancient world, the pursuit of enhancement was often mystical, considered divine or alchemical in nature. Cultures sought remedies for ailments and sought to improve physical abilities through various means, including rituals, plants, and potions believed to hold transformative powers. Take, for instance, the myths of Prometheus, who gifted humanity fire—a symbol not just of physical warmth but also of knowledge and advancement. The quest for eternal youth, exemplified by the search for the Fountain of Youth, reflects the timeless human desire to extend life and enhance the bodily experience.

As humanity progressed into the industrial era and beyond, the nature of this desire began to evolve. With the advent of science and technology, the enhancement became less about mythical attributes and more about tangible improvements in the human condition. The late 19th century and the 20th century saw revolutionary changes in medicine and technology that laid the groundwork for modern enhancements. The creation of vaccines, anesthesia, and antibiotics showcased the potential of medical science to enhance human health and longevity. As these technologies developed, the narrative shifted: enhancement was now a matter of life and death, a critical pathway to achieving better living standards and health outcomes.

The latter half of the 20th century brought about a significant cultural shift as the fields of computer science, biotechnology, and robotics began to intertwine. With the burgeoning digital age, humanity found itself on the cusp of a transformation fueled by technological advancement. The rise of the internet and the burgeoning field of artificial intelligence opened new avenues for enhancement. People began to envision not only improvements to physical health but cognitive augmentation as well, where technology is not just a tool but a means to enhance and redefine what it means to be human. This also began to bring questions of identity and authenticity to the forefront —what remains of our humanity when we enhance our bodies and brains with technology?

Modern society still grapples with these concepts of enhancement, particularly as we stand at the edge of profound transforming technologies. Genetic editing technologies such as CRISPR enable not only the treatment of genetic disorders but open the door to rethinking human potential at a foundational level. The desire for enhancement spurs research into enhancing memory, emotional well-being, and even happiness itself, creating an intersection of psychology, neuroscience, and cybernetics. People no longer wish merely to live longer; they aspire to live better—more fulfilled, healthier, and more capable.

Social dynamics play an essential role in this complex equation. As cybernetic enhancements become more accessible, there emerges a dichotomy in the narrative of enhancement—an empowered elite, poised to leverage these advancements, versus a disenfranchised base, unable to partake in the journey toward a more enhanced existence. This creates a new set of ethical conundrums regarding access, societal improvement, and the implications of human enhancement. What does it mean for individuals who can enhance their cognitive abilities through neural implants while others struggle to navigate everyday life without such enhancements? Furthermore, the psychological implications of living in a society where enhancement becomes the norm also raise pressing questions around identity, self-worth, and societal expectation.

The contemporary desire for enhancement, propelled by technology, urges society to grapple with philosophical ramifications. What does being human mean in the context of augmentations? Do enhancements enhance or dilute our humanity? Can we define a 'natural' human experience, or is that definition itself a construct shaped by evolving values and technologies?

As we explore the human desire for enhancement, we recognize that it reflects our deepest aspirations—a longing for progress, innovation, and or transcendence. The confluence of human and machine represents a rich and complex narrative where enhancement fuels our dreams but also challenges our understanding of identity, connection, and what it means to live a meaningful, authentic life. Thus, the pursuit of enhancement remains a defining characteristic of the contemporary human experience, shaping not only our present but also the future of humanity. In understanding this desire, we embark on a critical examination of ourselves and the pathways we carve toward not just surviving but thriving in an age where the limits of what it means to be human are continuously redrawn.

2.2. Early Concepts and Inspirations

The quest to surpass the limitations of our biological existence can be traced back to an eclectic mix of science fiction and revolutionary scientific advancements. Early imaginings of technology's role in the human experience ignited a fertile ground for speculation about enhancement, laying a profound influence on contemporary thought surrounding cybernetics. This interplay between imagination and innovation has shaped the vision of what human augmentation could become; much of it is rooted in the visions of yesteryear.

Science fiction has long served as a canvas where humanity's dreams, fears, and possibilities converge. Writers like Jules Verne and H.G. Wells dared to imagine futures filled with mechanized wonders and biological enhancements. Works such as "The Invisible Man," published in 1897, grappled with themes of transformation and the consequences of wielding power through scientific means. These texts not only captured the imagination of their contemporary readers but also created a framework for understanding the complexities of technological empowerment, allowing them to explore the potential and pitfalls of blending biology with machinery.

By visualizing what was never before possible, these authors contributed fundamental ideas to the modern conception of cybernetics. Their narratives often preemptively raised ethical questions surrounding technological advancements—issues of identity, morality, and existence—that would shape discussions around enhancement for decades to come. As we inspect their early ideas of bodies augmented by technology, we recognize an intrinsic desire to explore the duality of human nature: the simultaneous longing for transcendence and the fear of losing our essence.

Alongside literature, early scientific discoveries laid a crucial foundation for modern enhancement. The advent of mechanized devices, such as prosthetics in the 19th century, heralded the beginning of a concrete intersection between human life and mechanical assistance. These devices showcased a tangible method for overcoming physical disabilities, embodying the essential human drive to improve. The flashy advancements in medicine, especially within the realms of surgery and artificial limbs, inspired further inquiry into how technology could not only aid but enhance the human experience.

Moreover, the works of pioneers like Norbert Wiener, who is credited with coining the term 'cybernetics,' framed the discussion around feedback loops and self-regulating systems. Wiener's theoretical explorations emphasized the communication and control inherent within both biological systems and machines, establishing a common language that would unite future thinkers and inventors in pursuit of a technologically augmented existence. Wiener's vision played kaleidoscopic tricks on society's imagination, differentiating human intelligence and machine intelligence in ways that would redefine our understanding of identity and operational capacity.

As the 20th century unfurled, the voice of science fiction became an accompaniment to groundbreaking research in fields such as genetics, computing, and neuroscience. With the advent of computers, authors like Isaac Asimov extrapolated the essence of human experience into the realm of robotics, positing societies where machines could think, communicate, and, in some scenarios, even surpass human intelligence. His work, particularly the "Robot" series, laid out a framework for understanding the potential integration of artificial intelligence with humanity and encouraged readers and scientists alike to ponder not just the capabilities but also the ethical ramifications of such fusions.

The intricate relationship between fiction and innovation reveals an essential narrative: the capacity of imagination to push the boundaries of scientific inquiry. The 1960s and 1970s witnessed a surge of interest in computer technology and its implications for cognitive enhancement. The establishment of early neural interfaces kernelled in culture—beginning with the concept of "brain-computer interfaces"—brought speculative dreams one step closer to reality. Visionaries speculating about human consciousness while intertwined with technology became crucial as they presented ideas on how machines could bridge the gap between thought and action, tapping into the depths of human capabilities and even integrating artificial enhancements.

Finally, as the turn of the millennium approached, biotechnological advances such as gene therapy and the human genome project began to unravel the very fabric of human existence. These advances constituted powerful reasons to revisit the earlier imaginations: if we could manipulate our genetic code, where would that lead us? Would it enhance our humanity or detract from it altogether? The marketplace of ideas saw a dynamic interplay between science fiction themes and real-world research developments, forcing society to face pressing questions surrounding enhancement and identity.

The cultural tapestry woven by early scientific achievements and the speculative visions of future possibilities set the stage for an explosion of interest in cybernetic enhancements. The inspirations that traversed literature, ethics, and scientific breakthroughs culminated in a profound exploration of what it means to navigate an enhanced existence in a world where human ability is constantly being recalibrated by technology. As this narrative unfolds, we find ourselves at the precipice of technological transformation, where the insights of yesterday serve as guiding stars, illuminating the path toward a future where the boundaries of what it means to be human are increasingly elastic. Through this exploration, we unlock not only the potential for extraordinary enhancements but also the challenges that come with redefining our existence in a world irrevocably altered by our creativity, ambition, and imagination.

2.3. From Imagination to Innovation

The journey from fleeting thoughts and bold visions in speculative fiction to tangible technological advancements represents a fascinating narrative of human creativity and ingenuity, a narrative that continues to unfold in myriad directions. Throughout history, artists, writers, scientists, and philosophers have harnessed their imaginations to explore how technology might enhance or redefine the human experience. This dynamic interplay between imagination and innovation has played a pivotal role in shaping the developments we now classify as cybernetic enhancements.

As early as the 19th century, science fiction began to play a critical role in envisioning futures where technology could alter human capabilities. Works of fiction acted as thought experiments where authors posed essential questions about the essence of humanity, identity, and morality. These creative expressions were not merely escapist tales; they provided fertile ground for the birth of concepts that would resonate deeply within the scientific community. Authors like Mary Shelley with "Frankenstein" and Karel Čapek with "R.U.R" (Rossum's Universal Robots) introduced complex notions about creation, autonomy, and the potential perils of technological advancement. Shelley's cautionary tale about the consequences of unchecked innovation and Čapek's exploration of what it means to be human in a world populated with artificial beings forced readers and thinkers alike to grapple with profound questions long before tangible advancements in technology emerged.

The power of imagination in prompting scientific inquiry cannot be underestimated. Following the visionaries of speculative fiction, real-world scientific endeavors began to align with the themes explored in narratives. The invention of the telegraph, telephone, and eventually the computer set the stage for rapid digitization, as humanity sought to bridge communication gaps and redefine interactions. Inventors and engineers, inspired by earlier narratives, utilized these conceptual frameworks to propel their inventions. The idea of human-operated machines, much chronicled in science fiction, began to manifest itself through technological advancements such as mechanical prosthetics and, later, sophisticated robotics.

Entering the latter half of the 20th century, the concepts of cybernetics introduced by Norbert Wiener began gaining traction within both academic and popular spheres. Wiener's notion of communication and control systems provided a new lens through which inventors and scientists could view the interplay between human and machine. He envisioned a world where technology could not only assist but augment human capabilities. This sparked a wave of innovation in feedback systems and self-regulating machines, leading to explorations in artificial intelligence and machine learning. These investigations into machine functionality echoed the earlier fictional inquiries, posing essential questions about consciousness, thought, and the eventual merging of human and artificial intelligence.

As new computing technologies emerged in the late 20th century, combining mechanical innovation with burgeoning knowledge in biology, the conceptual landscape began to shift markedly. Visionaries such as Douglas Engelbart and Ivan Sutherland pushed the boundaries of what technology could do to augment human interaction and cognition. Engelbart's work on interactive computing and hypertext laid the groundwork for the internet, fundamentally changing how we communicate, share information, and collaborate across colossal distances. Sutherland's pioneering work on virtual reality opened new doors to experiential enhancements that would allow individuals to transcend their physical limitations.

Throughout the 21st century, rapid advancements in biotechnology and neuroscience have transformed ideas once deemed the realm of fiction into the forefront of scientific exploration. Technologies like CRISPR gene editing showcase the remarkable potential of molecular tools engineered to enhance human biology at a genetic level. This revolutionary capability, once the stuff of dreams, empowers researchers to contemplate heretofore unimaginable modifications, raising questions about ethical boundaries and the very fabric of human identity. The exploration of these territories reflects the intertwined narratives of imagination and innovation, where creative foresight leads the way into new scientific realms.

Moreover, we are witnessing an explosion of neuroscience-related technologies that promise to extend the capabilities of the human brain. Concepts like brain-computer interfaces, initially envisioned in speculative realms, are now challenging our understanding of cognition and consciousness, prompting a reconsideration of how thoughts and actions might intertwine with technology. The idea of augmenting our cognitive capabilities has become a hotbed of research and development, supported by breakthroughs in neurotechnology, which are pushing the envelope on how we can refine and enhance our innate abilities.

As we navigate this exhilarating landscape, it is crucial to recall that imagination is not a mere precursor to innovation but rather an integral part of the ongoing dialogue that shapes technology's trajectory. Each discovery contributes to an expanding continuum that transforms the speculative into the substantive, as society actively engages with the possibilities offered by new advancements. Innovation is not just about invention; it is also about reimagining humanity's relationship with technology and understanding the potential impacts and limitations of those innovations in real-world contexts.

In conclusion, the evolution from imagination to innovation within the realm of cybernetic enhancements reflects humanity's enduring pursuit of progress. What began as fanciful storytelling has blossomed into genuine scientific advancement. Yet, every technological leap beckons more questions—ethical dilemmas arise, societal divides reflect disparities in access, and philosophical inquiries into identity challenge our understanding of what it means to be human. The interplay between speculative visions and technological realities holds a mirror to our aspirations, desires, and the nature of our existence. As we stand at the precipice of further innovations yet to come, we must continue to ask not just how we can enhance ourselves but what it truly means to augment the human experience.

2.4. Visionaries Who Shaped a Movement

The exploration of cybernetic enhancements is intricate, and its roots trace back to several key visionaries whose ideas and inventions acted as catalysts for the movement toward a future where the fusion of human and machine becomes a defining characteristic of our existence. These pioneers have not only pushed the boundaries of technology but have also posed profound questions about the essence of humanity, the ethical implications of enhancement, and the direction of societal evolution. As we delve into their contributions, we begin to appreciate how their imaginative foresight has shaped our contemporary understanding of what it means to augment our existence.

One of the earliest and most influential figures in the development of cybernetics was Norbert Wiener, a mathematician and philosopher, who is considered the father of the field. In the 1940s, Wiener articulated the concept of feedback mechanisms within biological and mechanical systems, positing that both realms share a fundamental relationship. His seminal work, "Cybernetics: Or Control and Communication in the Animal and the Machine," bridged multiple disciplines, including engineering, biology, and psychology, presenting a vision of a world where machines could work in symbiosis with human beings. Wiener's insights laid the groundwork for the idea that machines could enhance human capabilities, leading to discussions on the ethical implications of such advancements. By framing the conversation around the interconnectedness of living systems and machines, Wiener created a conceptual foundation that continues to inform the discourse on technological enhancements today.

Building upon the ideas of Wiener and contemporaneous thought, figures like Douglas Engelbart pioneered advancements in human-computer interaction during the 1960s. Engelbart envisioned a future in which computers could augment human intelligence and collaborative capabilities. He developed the "oN-Line System" (NLS), which introduced the mouse and hypertext, fundamentally changing how individuals interacted with machines and each other. Engelbart's approach articulated the potential for technology to enhance cognitive processes, establishing the idea that by leveraging technological tools, we could transcend our innate limitations and improve our problem-solving abilities. His famous demonstration of the computer in 1968, which showcased various tools designed to augment human intellect, ignited interest in the transformative possibilities of these technologies.

At the intersection of fiction and innovation, we must also acknowledge the role of visionary authors such as Isaac Asimov and Arthur C. Clarke. Asimov's Robot series examined ethical dilemmas associated with artificial intelligence, shaping the narrative surrounding the coexistence of humans and machines. In his works, the notion of "The Three Laws of Robotics" instigated discussions regarding the moral frameworks necessary to govern interactions between humans and their creations. Meanwhile, Clarke, with visionary notions of satellite communication and space exploration, inspired generations of engineers and scientists to pursue technological feats that once seemed unattainable. Their contributions opened avenues not just for innovative technology but also for the cultural understanding surrounding enhancements, weaving complex moral fabrics into the fabric of human-machine interaction.

Moving into the realm of biology and enhancement, we encounter a pivotal figure such as Kevin Warwick, a cybernetics researcher often called "Captain Cyborg." Warwick's experiments with neural implants and communication between his nervous system and robotic devices exemplified an ambitious venture into human enhancement through direct interfacing with technology. His pioneering work demonstrated the prospect of merging the neurological aspects of being human with mechanical functionalities, thereby allowing for a rethinking of human capabilities. Warwick's experiments also raised critical ethical questions about identity and the implications of bodily modifications, inviting society to grapple with notions of authenticity in an increasingly cybernetic world.

As our understanding has evolved, newer visionaries, including pioneers in genetic engineering like Jennifer Doudna and Emmanuelle Charpentier, have significantly impacted the trajectory of cybernetic enhancements. Their groundbreaking work on CRISPR technology presents powerful possibilities for human enhancement at a genetic level. By providing tools to edit genes with unprecedented precision, the capabilities of CRISPR offer potential treatments for genetic diseases and discussions about the ethical implications of altering the human genome. This technology evokes a new era of enhancement debates: Should we pursue the ability to design enhanced traits within future generations? What responsibilities do we carry as we redefine what it is to be human at a biological level?

Another visionary in the arena of neurotechnology is Miguel Nicolelis, who has spent considerable effort in bridging brain-machine interfaces. His work in creating devices that allow paralyzed individuals to control robotic limbs through thought serves as a poignant reminder of the potential human enhancement has to alter lives dramatically. Nicolelis's research not only reflects advancements in prosthetic technology but also poses existential questions about consciousness, the nature of desire, and the extent to which we can control machinery through mental commands. His endeavors illustrate a remarkable merging of biology and technology, encouraging a future where technology is both an extension of ourselves and a redefinition of our capabilities.

Furthermore, the 21st century has seen a convergence of ideas that champions collective intelligence, drawing inspiration from the concept of hive consciousness. Innovators such as Jaron Lanier have challenged traditional notions of individuality through his advocacy for harnessing collaborative technologies. The potential to integrate thought processes within shared networks posits profound possibilities for human advancement. By working cooperatively, there emerges an avenue to address complex challenges facing society today—issues such as climate change, disease, and social injustice—fostering a vision of technological integration that emphasizes unity in enhancement.

As we chronicle the work of these visionaries, we discern an underlying theme threading through their contributions: the coexistence of ingenuity and ethical contemplation as society ventures toward an increasingly enhanced existence. From Wiener's dissemination of cybernetic principles to Warwick's experimental interfaces and the groundbreaking leaps in genetic editing facilitated by Doudna and Charpentier, each interaction between human desires for enhancement and the consequential ethical complexities offers a roadmap for navigating our future.

The journey is fraught with competing interests, aspirations, and philosophical dilemmas: where do we draw the line between beneficial enhancements and existential threats? As pioneers, these visionaries have initiated an expansive conversation encompassing biotechnology, ethics, philosophy, and human rights. Their legacies remind us that as we stand on the cusp of technological revolution, our engagement must not only focus on innovation itself but also on the implications of our decisions as we shape the contours of a future deeply interwoven with machines. In this domain, the role of visionaries is as much about dreaming up possibilities as it is about responsibly stewarding the movement towards merging with machines, ensuring that humanity retains its essence amid the alluring prospects of enhancement. Thus, we embark on a profound exploration of how the influence of these trailblazers not only sparks the transformative cycle of augmentation but redefines the very nature of what it means to be human in an age of technological co-evolution.

3. Breaking Biological Barriers

3.1. Understanding the Human Machine

In examining the intricacies of human biology through the lens of technology, we embark on a compelling journey that reveals the complexity of our physiological systems and how they can be enhanced by innovative mechanization and digital integration. Understanding the human machine requires a multi-faceted approach, delving into biological structures, neural mechanisms, and the demand for improvement that drives the pursuit of cybernetic enhancements. As we navigate this exploration, we focus on the interactions between biological processes and technological advancements that promise to reshape the human experience.

At the heart of our biological machinery lies a complex web of interconnected systems that allow us to function—each component finely tuned for optimal performance. The nervous system, responsible for transmitting signals throughout the body, comprises the brain, spinal cord, and a vast network of nerves. This intricate system not only regulates motor functions but also processes sensory information, orchestrates hormonal responses, and governs cognitive activities, forming the foundation of our interactions with the world. The way we interpret stimuli, express emotions, and respond to our environment is inherently tied to the efficiency of this biological framework.

With advancements in technology, we are increasingly poised to augment these biological processes. The development of wearable sensors, for instance, has enabled individuals to monitor physiological parameters such as heart rate, oxygen saturation, and even glucose levels in real time. These devices not only enhance our awareness of our bodily functions but also offer tailored interventions—whether it be through reminders to exercise, alerts about irregular heartbeats, or mechanisms for managing chronic conditions. The interplay between technology and biology offers a dualism—where we not only observe our biological state but also engage it through modifications facilitated by technological means.

Delving further into our understanding of the human machine involves considering how technology has evolved to interact with the brain—a crucial component in the enhancement narrative. Neurotechnology stands at the forefront of this discussion, where advancements such as brain-computer interfaces (BCIs) reveal the potential to meditate thought into action, bypassing traditional motor functions. Pioneering work in the field has illuminated pathways for individuals with mobility impairments to control robotic limbs merely by thinking. This revolutionary interaction showcases technology's ability to transcend human limitations, manifesting a direct connection between neural activity and machine behavior.

Moreover, as we delve deeper into cognitive enhancements, we encounter neurostimulation devices designed to boost mental faculties, such as memory, concentration, and learning speeds. These interventions, ranging from transcranial magnetic stimulation (TMS) to neurofeedback, aim to rewire neural pathways, fostering increased cognitive performance and emotional regulation. Importantly, these enhancements pose compelling questions surrounding identity, agency, and the nature of our thoughts and emotions—essentially coaxing us to reconsider what it means to be human in an age where our cognitive capabilities can be modified at will.

The human sensory apparatus presents yet another domain where technological advancements are paving the way for enhanced capabilities. Innovations in auditory and visual technologies, from cochlear implants to augmented reality devices, challenge the boundaries of natural perception. These devices serve dual functions—restoring lost functionalities to individuals with sensory impairments and amplifying sensory experiences for those without disabilities. For instance, augmented reality can superimpose digital information onto our visual field, enhancing our understanding of environments and tasks—transforming the way we interact with the physical world around us.

The promise of biotechnology does not stop at merely restoring lost capacities; it pushes into the realm of enhancement itself. Genetic engineering introduces pathways for augmenting the human body at a foundational level. Techniques such as CRISPR aim not only to correct genetic disorders but also extend the boundaries of human potential, allowing us to imagine the manipulation of traits that define our characteristics, from physical endurance to cognitive aptitude. This raises ethical dilemmas contrasting natural evolution against engineered progress, as society grapples with the implications of modifying the very essence of our biological identity.

While the drive toward enhancement is fueled by our desire for improvement, it is crucial to engage critically with the disparities these advancements may create. The accessibility of technology influences who benefits from enhancements and who finds themselves excluded from these opportunities. The widening gap between those with access to cutting-edge enhancements and those who do not presents profound societal implications. Questions of equity, ethics, and social justice emerge, as we must consider who gets to utilize these technologies and how they redefine societal norms concerning ability, intelligence, and health.

In contemplating the trajectory of enhancing the human machine, we recognize that the fusion of biology and technology is a dynamic interplay—an ongoing dialogue that asks us to reconsider not only our capabilities but our very definitions of humanity. As we explore the frameworks of our biological systems and the potential modifications that technology offers, we are led to reflect on profound philosophical questions: What augmentation should be pursued, and what ramifications will it entail for identity, society, and our future? The path toward enhancement beckons us, offering a promise laced with complexity, as we stand on the precipice of reconfiguring what it means to be human in an increasingly mechanized world. Each innovation not only rewrites the narrative of possibility but also reshapes our understanding of ourselves and the legacies we leave behind.

3.2. Revolutionary Biotechnologies

In recent years, we have witnessed a revolutionary shift in our understanding and manipulation of biological systems, driven by a combination of visionary exploration and technological advancements. The fusion of biology and cutting-edge technology has birthed an array of transformative biotechnologies that not only push the limits of what our bodies can achieve but also challenge our fundamental perceptions of health, enhancement, and identity. This compelling narrative begins with genetic engineering, notably exemplified by the CRISPR-Cas9 system, a groundbreaking tool that has redefined our approach to genetic modification.

CRISPR, originally discovered as a natural defense mechanism in bacteria against viruses, has emerged as a powerful tool for editing genes with unprecedented precision. By allowing scientists to target and modify specific sequences of DNA, CRISPR opens the door to a new era of genetic intervention—one where genetic disorders can be corrected, traits can be enhanced, and the very foundation of our biological makeup can be reimagined. It is a technology that holds immense promise for treating heritable diseases, eradicating genetic defects, and potentially enhancing attributes such as strength, intelligence, or resilience. However, the ethical implications of such capabilities remain a contentious topic that demands careful consideration. Should we edit the human genome to enhance the next generation, and what moral obligations do we hold toward those whose genes remain unedited?

Apart from genetic editing, the realm of bioprinting represents another frontier in revolutionary biotechnology. This innovative process employs 3D printing technologies to create tissue structures with living cells, effectively allowing for the construction of human organs on demand. Bioprinting has the potential to address one of the most pressing challenges in medicine: the scarcity of donor organs. By reducing waiting times and increasing the availability of transplantable organs, bioprinted tissues could save countless lives. This technology is not only revolutionary in its applications for regenerative medicine but also raises questions about the commercialization of life and the ethical concerns surrounding the creation of living tissues. As we move towards a future where organ printing becomes a reality, we must engage with complex narratives about the ownership of biotechnological creations and the implications for healthcare equity.

Synthetic biology is yet another field that is expanding our view of life itself. This interdisciplinary branch of science merges biology, engineering, and computer science to construct new biological parts, devices, and systems. By designing and constructing organisms with tailored functionalities, synthetic biology allows scientists to develop microorganisms programmed to perform specific tasks, such as producing biofuels, pharmaceuticals, or even environmental remediation agents. The implications of this technology are vast, ranging from improving agricultural yields to addressing climate change through engineered microbes capable of absorbing carbon dioxide. However, as with other transformative biotechnologies, synthetic biology does not come without risks. The manipulation of ecosystems and the introduction of synthetically created organisms into natural environments pose significant ethical and ecological questions that society must grapple with.

Artificial organs, prosthetics, and implants form another significant aspect of revolutionary biotechnologies, aiming to augment and enhance human capabilities. In the realm of medical devices, advancements such as neural implants, bionic limbs, and artificial retinas are transforming rehabilitation and enhancing quality of life for individuals with disabilities. These technologies exemplify the confluence of medicine and engineering, showcasing how artificial constructs can seamlessly integrate with human biological systems to restore lost functionalities and even enhance existing ones. Bionic limbs that respond to neural signals empower amputees to regain mobility and dexterity, while advancements in neuroprosthetics facilitate direct brain-machine interfacing, allowing for more nuanced control of prosthetic devices.

Wearable technologies are also reshaping how we view health and performance optimization. Devices capable of tracking physiological metrics such as heart rate, sleep patterns, and even stress levels offer users insights into their health status, fostering a proactive approach to wellness. As wearable technology advances, we are on the cusp of an era where continuous monitoring provides personalized feedback, enabling individuals to make informed decisions about their health and lifestyle. This personal data, when seamlessly analyzed and interpreted, could contribute to a societal shift toward preventive care and individualized health strategies, potentially reducing the burden on healthcare systems.

As we forge ahead into this exciting new frontier of biotechnology, it is essential to acknowledge the accompanying societal implications. The advancements we are witnessing evoke vital questions regarding access, equity, and the potential consequences of creating a world where enhancements are available primarily to those who can afford them. The prospect of a two-tiered society—one of enhanced individuals and another of those unable to access these technologies—demands a robust ethical framework that emphasizes inclusivity and equitable access to biotechnology.

Ethical considerations surrounding consent, genetic privacy, and the potential for unintended consequences also loom large in the discussion of revolutionary biotechnologies. Should individuals be allowed to modify their own genetic code, and how do we safeguard against misuse of such powerful technologies? With advancements enabling us to change our biological destiny on such a fundamental level, society must navigate the complexities of consent, ensuring that individuals are fully informed about the implications of genetic editing and modification.

In summary, the landscape of revolutionary biotechnologies represents an extraordinary convergence of human ingenuity, scientific advancement, and ethical inquiry. As we explore the implications of CRISPR, bioprinting, synthetic biology, artificial organs, and wearable technologies, we stand at the threshold of a new era where the boundaries of human potential are being redefined. Navigating the challenges and opportunities presented by these biotechnologies is crucial as we puzzle together the visions of what it means to enhance our existence while maintaining our core human identity. The future beckons, promising extraordinary possibilities that demand careful reflection, active dialogue, and a collective commitment to ensure that all individuals can benefit from the transformative power of biotechnology in an equitable and ethical manner.

3.3. Neurotechnology: Beyond Brainpower

In an era characterized by remarkable advancements in neuroscience and biotechnology, the goal of transcending the cognitive constraints of the human brain is increasingly becoming a reality. Neurotechnology, a field that bridges the gap between neuroscience and technology, is propelling us toward the potential of artificial enhancements aimed at improving cognitive functions. These developments not only promise to expand our mental capacities beyond conventional limits but also underscore critical ethical, philosophical, and societal implications on the future of what it means to be human.

One of the most significant breakthroughs in neurotechnology is the development of brain-computer interfaces (BCIs). BCIs offer a direct communication pathway between the brain and external devices, enabling individuals to control computers or prosthetic limbs through thoughts alone. By interpreting neural signals, these interfaces unlock a myriad of applications, particularly for individuals with disabilities, enabling them to regain agency and functionality in ways previously thought impossible. Beyond restoration, BCIs hint at a future where augmented cognition becomes a possibility. Enhancing motor functions is merely the beginning; researchers are exploring how to interpret complex brain signals to facilitate tasks like learning, memory enhancement, and even emotional regulation.

Current innovations in neurostimulation techniques, such as transcranial direct current stimulation (tDCS) and deep brain stimulation (DBS), represent another avenue toward cognitive enhancement. By applying electrical stimulation to specific areas of the brain, these methods have shown promise in improving memory, learning new skills, and potentially alleviating symptoms of mental health disorders. The ability to modulate brain activity through targeted electrical currents could lead to a new era in education and cognitive training, shooting beyond traditional methods to create neurological pathways that bolster intellectual prowess. Imagine a world where one can acquire knowledge far more efficiently and retain it indefinitely—transforming the very nature of education and lifelong learning.

Yet, while the excitement surrounding neurotechnology is palpable, it compels us to confront the ethical dilemmas tied to such enhancements. The idea of augmenting intelligence raises questions about equity—who benefits from these advancements? If cognitive enhancements become accessible only to the wealthy, could we widen the already significant gap between socioeconomic classes, leading to a society divided between the cognitively enhanced and the unenhanced? Additionally, we must consider the potential for coercion as cognitive enhancements gain traction in competitive job markets. Would individuals feel pressured to undergo enhancement procedures to remain relevant in their fields, and how would that reshape our understanding of meritocracy?

Moreover, the implications of identity cannot be understated. As we venture into territories where cognitive abilities can be changed or optimized, we confront questions about personal identity and authenticity. What does it mean to be intelligent, and can the essence of our intellectual capacity be quantitatively altered? Neurological enhancements beg the inquiry—how much of our identity is tied to our natural cognitive capacities, and at what point do enhancements become alterations of the self? In a world where intelligence is enhanced logarithmically, could we be losing aspects of what it means to think, feel, and learn as distinctly human experiences?

Exploration into enhancing memory and cognitive function also points to profound implications for mental health. Neurotechnology holds promise to revolutionize the treatment landscape for conditions such as anxiety, depression, and PTSD. Utilizing techniques like neurofeedback, which trains individuals to alter their brain states through real-time feedback, we may nurture a generation more adept at managing emotional and psychological challenges. Furthermore, the therapeutic use of psychedelics and their integration with technology opens discussions around using neurotechnology in mental health treatments, creating pathways toward healing and self-discovery in transformative ways.

In summary, the advancements in neurotechnology that seek to exceed the cognitive limitations of the human brain offer astounding potential for enhancement across various domains—from education to personal development and mental health. However, as we stand on the precipice of these technological transformations, we must navigate a complex landscape fraught with ethical considerations. The prospect of cognitive enhancement invites us to reflect critically on identity, access, and our conception of what it means to be human in an age of machines. As these technologies evolve, it will ultimately be our responsibility to ensure that they serve to enrich humanity while preserving the core values and ethics that define our existence. The conversation surrounding neurotechnology is not merely about what we can do but also about what we ought to do, as we embrace the possibilities that lie before us.

3.4. Augmenting the Senses

In the rapidly evolving landscape of human augmentation, sensory technology stands out as a particularly fascinating area of innovation. The quest to expand human perception beyond our natural capabilities has given rise to an impressive array of tools and devices designed to enhance the way we experience the world. From auditory enhancements to augmented visual systems, innovations in sensory technology hold untold potential to reshape our interactions with our surroundings and redefine what it means to perceive reality.

One of the most significant advancements in sensory technology is the development of auditory devices aimed at the enhancement of hearing. Cochlear implants have transformed the lives of individuals with significant hearing impairments, allowing them to perceive sound with greater clarity than ever before. These devices work by converting sound waves into electrical signals, which are then transmitted directly to the auditory nerve, bypassing damaged portions of the ear. The result is a profound change in communication and social engagement for those who, prior to receiving implants, may have struggled with auditory processing. Research is ongoing to develop next-generation auditory enhancements that promise improvements in sound localization and tonal discrimination, enabling a more immersive auditory experience.

Furthermore, hearing enhancements are not limited to medical interventions. Emerging technologies like smart hearing aids and earbuds are tailored to improve auditory experiences in everyday contexts. These devices optimize audio environments by filtering out background noise while amplifying specific sounds, creating personalized auditory landscapes that cater to individual preferences and environments. By leveraging artificial intelligence, these devices can learn user preferences over time, making them adaptable companions in various settings, from crowded conference halls to serene natural landscapes. Such enhancements allow users not only to enjoy music, podcasts, and conversations but also to enhance their awareness of surroundings, serving as a bridge to a more connected existence.

On the visual spectrum, augmented reality (AR) technologies represent a monumental leap in expanding human perception. By overlaying digital information onto the physical world, AR systems allow users to experience enhanced visual landscapes brimming with interactive and contextual information. Applications range from educational tools that enhance learning by providing visual aids and simulations, to navigation systems that project directional information directly onto the real world, facilitating smoother and more intuitive travel experiences. These developments diminish the barriers between digital and physical realms, deepening immersion in both learning and exploration.

Envision the future where AR integrates seamlessly into our daily lives, facilitating tasks like cooking with step-by-step interactive guides projected onto countertops, or allowing remote collaboration where participants can visualize and manipulate digital objects as if they are physically present. These applications not only elevate personal experiences but can also transform industries in areas like healthcare training, design, and entertainment, pushing the boundaries of how we interact with our environments and with each other.

The realm of olfactory innovations is another exciting frontier. Research is currently exploring how scent can be artificially enhanced or even digitally transmitted to create multisensory experiences. Beyond mere fragrance diffusion, this field delves into emotional connectivity to scent, recognizing the profound impact that olfactory stimuli can have on memory and mood. Future innovations may allow individuals to curate personalized scent experiences that influence their emotional states, utilizing technology that synthesizes and delivers scent in targeted environments. This could open avenues for applications in therapeutic settings, as scents known to alleviate stress or induce relaxation can be strategically deployed in various contexts.

Moreover, technology aimed at enhancing tactile sensations is also emerging, with innovations such as wearable haptic devices designed to convey tactile feedback. These devices allow users to experience touch-based interactions in virtual environments, enriching the experience of gaming, education, or rehabilitation. Imagine a virtual reality program that not only immerses the user in a visual landscape but also provides realistic touch sensations, allowing them to feel the texture of surfaces or the impact of interactions. Such technology could significantly enhance learning experiences or therapeutic applications aimed at helping those with tactile sensory processing disorders, thereby transforming the way we receive and process information.

The interplay of sensory technologies also extends to the integration of multisensory experiences through neural interfaces. As we forge deeper connections between human cognition and technology, researchers are exploring methods to calibrate sensory inputs directly into the brain, resulting in a level of interaction far beyond what traditional enhancements can offer. These innovations, employing neural modulation and stimulation techniques, promise possibilities where individuals can access augmented sensory information directly from their cognitive processors, heightening sensitivity or enabling entirely new forms of perception such as infrared vision or sonar-like echolocation.

With the proliferation of sensory enhancements emerges a new discourse on the ethical implications of such technologies. As sensory capabilities expand, questions surrounding identity, accessibility, and authenticity take center stage. Who has the right to access these enhancements? As we enhance our senses, how do we ensure that we maintain a shared experience of reality? The potential for disparities to arise based on access to augmented sensory technologies raises concerns over socio-economic divides: the opportunity to perceive the world in new ways may become a privilege rather than a universal right. Ensuring equitable access to sensory enhancements will be paramount as we advance further into this transformative landscape.

Additionally, the integration of augmented sensory experiences will necessitate a re-evaluation of societal norms and expectations regarding sensory perception. As our abilities to perceive the world undergo radical recalibrations, traditional definitions of normalcy may be challenged. A future where augmented sensory experiences are commonplace could lead us to rethink what constitutes disability, ability, and even human connection.

As we look toward the horizon of augmenting human senses, we find ourselves at a fascinating intersection where technology and biology converge. The innovations in sensory technology promise not only to expand our perceptions but also to redefine how we engage with our world, ourselves, and each other. The journey ahead invites us to navigate a landscape rich with transformative possibilities, raising essential questions regarding our individuality, connections, and the very fabric of our shared human experience. In this endeavor, we reinforce the necessity for ethical considerations to accompany our rapid advancements, fostering a future where enhanced perception serves as a bridge that deepens our understanding of what it means to be human in the face of boundless technological potential.

3.5. Biological Versus Artificial Enhancements

The discourse surrounding human enhancements has evolved into a rich tapestry woven from the threads of biology and machine technology, each possessing unique merits and challenges. Biological enhancements, derived from natural systems, offer a compelling narrative of evolution and adaptation. Meanwhile, artificial enhancements, born from innovation and engineering, introduce possibilities that challenge our very understanding of human limitation. As society stands at the crossroads of these two paradigms, it becomes imperative to contemplate the implications of each approach, weighing their benefits, ethical considerations, and overarching societal impact.

Biological enhancements refer to physiological and genetic modifications that leverage the body's own systems to increase resilience, improve health outcomes, or augment capabilities. Transformative advances in genetic engineering, particularly technologies like CRISPR, exemplify the potential of harnessing biological processes to transcend human limitations. Within the realm of regenerative medicine, the use of stem cells and tissue engineering aims to bolster the body's natural healing capacities, potentially allowing individuals to regenerate damaged organs or tissues. Such enhancements often evoke a sense of authenticity, tying back to the age-old human quest for improvement while aligning with the inherent biological fabric of our existence.

One of the primary merits of biological enhancements lies in their compatibility with natural systems. By working within the body's established frameworks, these enhancements may produce fewer rejection responses or complications, establishing a smoother integration process. The body is designed to thrive on its own, and enhancing it biologically is often perceived as a natural progression of human evolution—a continuation of the adaptive journey shaped by millennia of environmental pressures.

However, biological enhancements are not without challenges. The ethical considerations surrounding genetic editing raise critical questions about consent, the potential for eugenics, and the implications for future generations. The very ability to manipulate genetic sequences poses profound dilemmas regarding "playing God." Determining the parameters of what constitutes an acceptable enhancement versus an unacceptable alteration becomes an arduous, if not insurmountable, task.

In stark contrast, artificial enhancements encapsulate a technological approach that seeks to expand human capabilities through devices, systems, and synthetic materials. From neural implants that enhance cognitive functions to bionic limbs that outdo natural anatomy in speed and strength, artificial enhancements promise radical upgrades that are not inherently limited by biological viability. This approach reflects human ingenuity, demonstrating a desire to leverage technology to overcome the limitations of the human condition.

The key benefits of artificial enhancements lie in their potentials for dramatic amplification of human capabilities. For instance, exoskeleton suits can empower individuals with mobility challenges, allowing them to walk and navigate spaces previously inaccessible. Underpinning this is the notion that technology does not simply replicate human function; it aims to enhance it to levels previously unimaginable. In environments where biological limitations present significant barriers, artificial enhancements open doors to infinite possibilities.

However, the pursuit of artificial enhancements presents its own ethical challenges. Issues of identity and authenticity loom large; as individuals augment themselves through machines, questions arise about the integrity of the self. What remains of our humanity when we enhance or replace natural processes with artificial counterparts? Furthermore, the potential for socio-economic polarization emerges as a critical consideration. If access to advanced enhancements becomes stratified by wealth and privilege, society may veer into a reality where enhanced individuals are marked by their divergence from natural humans, potentially leading to unforeseen ramifications of inequality and division.

In addition, the prospect of artificial enhancements necessitates a reevaluation of how society defines physical and cognitive capabilities. As augmented individuals excel beyond traditional limits, it raises urgent concerns on how achievements are assessed. If enhancements begin to set benchmarks for success, individuals who are not augmented may feel pressured to undergo enhancements, with their worth and potential being measured against synthetic capabilities.

Ultimately, navigating the dichotomy between biological and artificial enhancements leads us to grapple with a profound question: how do we define authenticity in a rapidly transforming world? The integration of enhancement technologies, whether biological or artificial, compels society to reflect on the essence of what it means to be human. It invites dialogue that transcends traditional definitions, acknowledging the fluidity and complexity of human identity in a society increasingly shaped by advancements.

As we explore the merits and challenges of each approach towards human enhancement, the focus must also extend to the ethical frameworks governing these innovations. The conversations surrounding access, equity, and authenticity must be dissected to illuminate pathways that ensure a holistic, inclusive approach to enhancement. Embracing a balanced perspective—one that celebrates the intersection of biological evolution and technological innovation—will empower humanity to walk the line between enhancement and authenticity, shaping a future where human potential is expanded without compromising the values that define our existence. Ultimately, this harmonious relationship between biologically rooted enhancements and innovative artificial solutions could lead to a reimagining of the human experience, opening new avenues for fulfillment and understanding in an ever-evolving landscape.

4. Collapsing the Digital Divide

4.1. The Internet of Things

In exploring the interconnected world of devices and systems that comprises the Internet of Things (IoT), we stand witness to a transformational shift in how we experience our environments, communicate, and augment our realities. Envision a vast ecosystem where everyday objects—from our homes to the vehicles we drive—are equipped with sensors, software, and connectivity. These elements work together to share and process data, creating a nexus of intelligence that enhances our interaction with the physical world. The Internet of Things illustrates the profound integration of digital technology into our lives, leading us toward a more interconnected existence where the notion of a standalone device is rapidly becoming obsolete.

At the heart of IoT lies the potential for continuous data exchange, fostering real-time interactions between users and their environments. Imagine a smart home system that learns your preferences and adjusts the heating, lighting, and security measures automatically, all while you remain blissfully unaware of the underlying complexity. This seamless exchange of information is driven by interconnected devices—smart thermostats, lighting systems, refrigerators, and security cameras—that collect data to optimize functionality and ensure comfort. The ability of these devices to communicate offers not just convenience but also energy efficiency and enhanced security protocols, as homeowners receive alerts about unusual activity and can monitor their homes from virtually anywhere.

The applications of IoT extend beyond domestic environments; they permeate various sectors, including healthcare, agriculture, transportation, and industry. Smart health devices, such as wearables that track vital signs, activity levels, and sleep patterns, provide invaluable data to both users and healthcare providers. This information enables preventive care and facilitates timely interventions, reducing the strain on healthcare systems while improving patient outcomes. In agriculture, IoT sensors monitor soil conditions, weather patterns, and crop health, allowing farmers to make data-driven decisions that optimize yields and conserve resources. The agricultural sector, often viewed as traditional and labor-intensive, is beginning to embrace a data-centric approach that enhances productivity while fostering sustainable practices.

Transportation exemplifies another area where the Internet of Things plays a critical role in reshaping industries. Consider the rise of smart vehicles equipped with sensors that monitor driving behavior, detect obstacles, and communicate with traffic management systems. These enhancements lead to improved safety and efficiency, as real-time data informs users about potential hazards, route optimizations, and vehicle performance metrics. As a result, we find not just individual vehicles that are smarter but entire transportation networks that operate cohesively to promote fluid movement and reduce congestion, contributing to overall urban efficiency.

With this integration of devices and systems, we also encounter the concept of smart cities—urban environments that leverage data and connectivity to improve living standards. Smart city initiatives encompass everything from traffic management systems that optimize flow and reduce emissions to intelligent waste management that monitors waste levels and adjusts collection routes accordingly. Through these technologies, civic authorities can enhance public services, foster sustainability, and ultimately improve residents' quality of life. The rise of smartphone applications that allow citizens to engage with municipal services further illustrates how IoT fosters collaborative communities where public input and real-time feedback enhance governance.

However, the rise of IoT does not come without challenges and concerns that merit thorough consideration. The vast amount of data generated by interconnected devices raises pressing questions about data privacy and security. As our lives become increasingly interconnected, the potential for cyber threats escalates, as malicious actors may seek to exploit vulnerabilities in these networks. Individuals and organizations must navigate a landscape where personal data is continuously collected, analyzed, and potentially misused, prompting robust discussions around data ownership and consent.

Equally pressing are the ethical implications surrounding the Internet of Things and its role in shaping our experiences. With devices learning our preferences and habits, how much autonomy do we retain in decision-making? As the lines blur between human agency and algorithmic influence, we must grapple with the philosophical questions inherent in relying on technology to augment the fabric of our lives. Furthermore, disparities in access to IoT technologies raise concerns about equity; as smart devices and systems become more prevalent, those without access may find themselves further marginalized, unable to participate in the digital ecosystem.

A critical facet of the Internet of Things is its role in personal augmentation—how can we harness these interconnected systems to enhance our capabilities as individuals? The data gathered through IoT provides insights into our behaviors and preferences, feeding personalized experiences that reflect our needs. Think about a fitness app that utilizes data from your wearable devices to suggest optimized workouts tailored to your daily activity levels and goals. Such applications not only encourage healthier lifestyles but empower individuals with the tools to make informed decisions about their well-being, potentially reshaping public health paradigms.

Moreover, as we contemplate the future of IoT, we find ourselves entering an era where the increase in interconnectedness will necessitate a greater focus on developing ethical frameworks that address the consequences of these advancements. Protections surrounding privacy and security will need to evolve parallel to the rapid technological developments, ensuring that individuals are not only safeguarded but also empowered in an ecosystem that continually shapes and defines their experiences.

In conclusion, the Internet of Things represents a confluence of technology and everyday existence, creating a vast digital ecosystem that augments and enhances our realities. As we navigate this interconnected landscape, we recognize both the extraordinary potential for personal augmentation and the accompanying challenges that necessitate thoughtful consideration. Balancing innovation with ethical responsibility will be crucial in shaping a future where technology enriches our lives while upholding our values and promoting equity. Through careful engagement with the Internet of Things, we can aspire to a world where the benefits of connectivity are shared widely, ultimately guiding humanity toward a more empowered and interconnected existence.

4.2. Big Data and Artificial Intelligence

Big data and artificial intelligence (AI) represent interconnected paradigms that reshape the landscape of personal augmentation and decision-making processes. In a world where the volume of data generated each day is staggering, harnessing this information through AI offers a pathway to not only enhance individual capabilities but also redefine operational frameworks across various domains of life. Understanding the relationship between big data and AI is essential as we explore how these technologies inform our choices and perceptions, ultimately crafting a more integrated and enhanced existence.

At the core of big data lies the aggregation of vast datasets collected from myriad sources—ranging from social media interactions and web searches to sensor technologies embedded in everyday objects. This data encompasses a wide spectrum of information: consumer preferences, environmental conditions, and even biometric metrics. The synthesis and analysis of this data present unprecedented opportunities to gain insights into human behavior, market trends, and emerging patterns. For individuals, the potential benefits of big data reside in customized experiences—recommendations for products, tailored marketing campaigns, and targeted content designed to engage users in ways that resonate with their interests.

Artificial intelligence plays a pivotal role in sifting through the noise inherent in big data. Machine learning algorithms intelligently analyze data, identifying correlations and recognizing patterns that would be imperceptible to human analysis. This forms the backbone of AI systems, which function to predict behavior, enhance user experience, and facilitate informed decision-making. In domains such as healthcare, AI-driven data analytics can measure patient health indicators, predict potential health risks, and recommend preventative measures, effectively providing a form of augmented insight for both practitioners and patients.

One prominent way in which big data and AI prioritize personal augmentation is through personalized learning experiences. In educational settings, AI systems analyze student performance data, learning styles, and engagement metrics to tailor educational content to meet individual needs. This adaptive learning environment attunes itself to the pace and preferences of each learner, maximizing retention and skill acquisition. Students are no longer confined to a one-size-fits-all curriculum; instead, they receive an enhanced educational experience that acknowledges their unique abilities and challenges.

Moreover, the interplay of big data and AI extends to the realm of mental and emotional well-being. AI-powered applications harness user-generated data from various tasks and interactions, ultimately identifying patterns relevant to mental health. For instance, mood-tracking apps analyze daily sentiments, enabling users to reflect on patterns and even predict emotional fluctuations. This knowledge equips individuals with tools and insights to enhance their mental resilience, fostering proactive approaches to well-being.

In the realm of consumer behavior, big data analysis allows companies to create personalized experiences that feel resonant and meaningful to individuals. By understanding preferences and behaviors in real-time, businesses can make data-driven decisions about product offerings, pricing strategies, and marketing campaigns. Consumers benefit from receiving targeted information and product suggestions that enhance their purchasing experiences, while businesses can optimize operational efficiency and marketing budgets.

However, the integration of big data and AI into our lives prompts important ethical considerations. These technologies operate on vast amounts of personal data, raising critical questions about privacy, consent, and data ownership. As users generate more data, they must navigate challenges around how their information is collected, utilized, and safeguarded. The potential for data misuse or manipulation amplifies concerns about the transparency of AI-driven processes and the extent to which individuals can influence how their data is employed.

The trust required for meaningful engagement with these technologies necessitates stringent frameworks for data protection—ensuring personal information remains secure and that users receive clear, informed choices regarding data usage. Achieving balance in leveraging big data's capabilities while respecting user privacy will be crucial as AI increasingly permeates personal and societal frameworks.

In cases where AI and big data converge in decision-making processes, we encounter the potential for algorithmic bias—situations where AI systems, influenced by flawed or incomplete data, may perpetuate inequities or stereotypes. Addressing these biases becomes paramount as we strive towards a fair, just, and inclusive technological future. Continuous assessment of algorithmic outcomes, diversity in training data, and inclusive development practices will be essential to mitigate the pitfalls inherent in AI systems.

In examining this dynamic interplay between big data and AI, we find ourselves at a unique juncture that emphasizes the promise of personal augmentation while demanding ethical vigilance. As individuals increasingly rely on data-driven insights to inform decisions across facets of daily life, embracing these advancements becomes essential. By enhancing our understanding of our choices and tailoring our experiences, we edge closer to realizing the full potential of an augmented existence, one defined by the seamless integration of technology into the human experience.

Ultimately, the relationship between big data and AI empowers individuals, enabling them to navigate the complexities of modern life with enhanced agency and informed decision-making. Yet, as we move forward, it is crucial to anchor these developments with ethical tandems, ensuring that the quest for augmentation does not compromise fundamental principles of privacy, equity, and humanity. Embracing this new paradigm will not only redefine our approach to personal enhancement but will shape the very essence of what it means to live in an increasingly interconnected world.

4.3. The Role of Robotics in Daily Life

As robots continue to evolve and increasingly integrate into various aspects of human life, their role serves as a testament to the transformative potential of technology in reshaping how we conduct our daily activities. These sophisticated machines are no longer confined to industrial factories or science fiction narratives; today, they are woven into the very fabric of our homes, workplaces, and social environments, demonstrating enhanced capabilities that can augment mundane tasks, provide companionship, and even assist in critical healthcare processes. This exploration delves into the multifaceted dimensions of robotic integration, highlighting their observable impacts across diverse settings, and uncovering the implications of their growing presence in our lives.

One of the most significant areas where robotics has made a considerable impact is healthcare. Robotic technologies are revolutionizing patient care, surgical procedures, and rehabilitation processes. Surgical robots, such as the da Vinci Surgical System, enable surgeons to perform minimally invasive surgeries with unparalleled precision and control. By facilitating tiny incisions and providing magnified views of the operating field, robotic-assisted surgery improves patient recovery times and minimizes complications. As surgeons increasingly adopt robotic platforms, the potential for enhanced surgical outcomes becomes part of the medical toolkit, signifying a shift toward more sophisticated methodologies in healthcare.

Beyond surgery, robots play a crucial role in patient care and rehabilitation through assistive technologies that enhance the quality of life for individuals with disabilities or chronic illnesses. Robotic exoskeletons empower individuals with mobility challenges to regain the ability to walk, promoting physical rehabilitation and independence. These devices use advanced sensor technology and artificial intelligence to respond to the wearer's movements, providing support and stability. The integration of robotics into rehabilitation offers hope for a new standard of care, emphasizing not only restoration but also the enhancement of human capabilities.

In addition to direct healthcare applications, robots have established themselves as invaluable companions in long-term care facilities. Socially assistive robots, designed to engage with patients emotionally and cognitively, provide interaction and companionship that can alleviate feelings of loneliness and isolation, particularly among the elderly. These robots use natural language processing and machine learning algorithms to interact with users, facilitating conversations, offering reminders for medication, and even engaging in games and activities. The emotional support they provide serves as a complement to traditional healthcare practices, highlighting how robotics can address not only physical but also psychosocial needs.

Home management is another domain ripe for robotic intervention, showcasing how automation can streamline everyday tasks. Robotic vacuum cleaners, like the Roomba, symbolize the domestic revolution, allowing individuals to maintain cleanliness in their homes with minimal effort. These robots utilize intelligent mapping systems and sensors to navigate around furniture, adapting to changing environments while ensuring efficient cleaning. The use of home automation technologies expands further with robotic lawnmowers, kitchen assistants, and smart appliances that enhance convenience, efficiency, and energy management within households.

The workplace is also experiencing significant transformation due to robotics. Collaborative robots, or cobots, have emerged as reliable partners in environments such as manufacturing and logistics. Unlike traditional industrial robots that often operate in isolation and require extensive safety measures, cobots are designed to work alongside human workers. They assist with repetitive or ergonomically challenging tasks, reducing workplace injuries and increasing productivity. This integration reflects a shift towards human-robot collaboration, fostering a work culture that elevates efficiency while preserving the essential human touch.

Moreover, advancements in artificial intelligence empower robots to adapt their behaviors and capabilities to fit specific contexts. Machine learning algorithms allow robots to learn from their experiences, improving their performance over time. This adaptability is crucial in settings such as personal assistants, where the robot can learn user preferences, routines, and needs, ultimately providing more personalized and effective support. Such responsiveness illuminates the future potential for robots to become integral components of our daily ecosystems, enhancing and tailoring their services to individual lifestyles.

As the role of robotics in daily life expands, it invites us to reflect on the broader implications of this integration. The potential for robots to free individuals from mundane tasks raises important questions regarding autonomy and labor. Automation promises increased efficiency and leisure, but it may lead to job displacement in sectors previously reliant on human labor. Society must grapple with how to balance the benefits of robotic capabilities with the implications for employment and economic structures.

Furthermore, the emotional and ethical dimensions of human-robot interaction warrant careful consideration. As robots assume more significant roles in caregiving and companionship, the nature of relationships and connections may evolve. The question arises: can a robot truly grasp empathy, and how does its presence affect human social dynamics? Navigating the ethical landscapes of robotics will require ongoing dialogue around the implications of creating machines that can simulate emotional responses and engage in social behaviors.

In conclusion, the role of robotics in daily life has evolved into a multifaceted phenomenon that spans healthcare, home management, and workplace environments. As robots continue to enhance human capabilities, their integration highlights both the potential benefits of automation and the ethical, social, and economic implications that unfold alongside it. Regular examination of our relationship with robotics will be essential as we progress toward a future where these technological companions reshape the contours of our existence, define our interactions, and augment our human experience in profound new ways.

4.4. Seamless Digital Integration

As we navigate the landscape of contemporary life, the integration of technology into our everyday existence becomes increasingly seamless, often occurring without us even recognizing its presence. This digital integration creates a state of harmony, where technology works in concert with human activities, enriching our experiences while minimizing disruption. In this exploration, we will delve into how such advancements manifest in various aspects of our lives and examine the implications they carry for our future.

The advent of smart devices exemplifies seamless digital integration, as these gadgets become commonplace in households, workplaces, and public spaces. Imagine waking up to a smart alarm clock that syncs with your sleep patterns, gently rousing you at the optimal time. As you rise, your coffee maker, connected to the internet, begins brewing the perfect cup of coffee based on your preferences, while your thermostat adjusts the temperature for maximum comfort. This early morning routine, orchestrated by intelligent devices, demonstrates the foundational premise of integration: technology that anticipates our needs, streamlining our tasks and enhancing our quality of life.

Moreover, the proliferation of wearables, such as fitness trackers and smartwatches, epitomizes this integration. These devices collect real-time data about our physical activities, heart rates, and even sleep quality, providing valuable feedback and fostering informed health decisions. The information gleaned from wearables informs users not only about their current state of well-being but can serve as a catalyst for lifestyle changes, including improved exercise habits and nutritional choices. Through the lens of personal health, seamless integration allows us to cultivate a proactive relationship with our bodies, empowering us to take charge of our health with minimal effort.

This blended existence continues through our social and professional interactions. The rise of digital communication platforms—be it video conferencing tools, collaborative workspaces, or instant messaging applications—has transformed how we connect, collaborate, and share information. In a world where hybrid work models are becoming the norm, these platforms allow teams to work together cohesively, regardless of geographic boundaries. The technologies aim to replicate and enhance in-person interactions, incorporating virtual backgrounds, real-time collaboration tools, and screen sharing features that enrich meetings and brainstorming sessions. The frictionless nature of these technologies fosters a fluid exchange of ideas, enabling creativity and productivity to thrive.

Nonetheless, the invisible integration of technology does not come without its challenges. The increasing reliance on digital systems raises important questions about data privacy and the implications of being perpetually connected. The very devices and applications that enhance our lives also collect vast amounts of personal data, often leading to concerns about surveillance, consent, and autonomy. As companies gather information to personalize our experiences, understanding the balance between convenience and privacy becomes paramount in sustaining trust in our digital interactions.

The digital landscape's evolution also underscores the significance of ethical considerations regarding accessibility. As these technologies become vital components of daily life, it is crucial to ensure equitable access across socio-economic divides. The risk of widening gaps between those who can utilize these advanced technologies and those who cannot poses a challenge to social equity. Creating an inclusive society requires a commitment to addressing disparities in access, ensuring that everyone can benefit from enhancements that promote holistic well-being.

Furthermore, the psychological implications of digital integration demand reflection. The presence of technology in every facet of life blurs the lines between human experiences and machine interactions. As we find ourselves increasingly reliant on devices for support, we must consider how these enhancements impact our mental health and sense of identity. The potential for over-dependence on technology raises critical questions about authenticity and the essence of human connection in an era defined by digital integration.

Looking ahead, the trajectory of seamless digital integration beckons an intriguing future, inviting us to ponder the boundaries of human experience. As technology continues to interplay with our daily lives, the idea of a harmonious existence shaped by digital advancements could redefine what it means to live authentically. The challenge lies in navigating this landscape responsibly, ensuring that the integration of technology serves to enhance human experiences rather than diminish them.

In conclusion, seamless digital integration represents a hallmark of our contemporary existence, reshaping how we live, work, and interact. While the benefits are crystal clear—efficiency, convenience, and enhanced quality of life—one cannot overlook the ethical considerations and challenges that accompany this transformation. As we integrate technology into the fabric of our lives, ongoing dialogue concerning access, privacy, and the psychological dimensions of our increasingly digital interactions will be essential. By fostering a framework that puts humanity at the center of these advancements, we can strive to create a future where technology elevates our human experiences, nurturing a harmonious coexistence between individuals and the intelligent systems that accompany them.

5. The Ethical Equation

5.1. Redefining the Norms of Humanity

The transformational journey of humanity, shaped by the advent of cybernetic enhancements, raises vital considerations about the very nature of what it means to be human. As technology intensifies its influence over our biological makeup, society stands at a crossroads —an intersection where traditional concepts of identity, morality, and culture are being redefined through the lens of enhancement.

Philosophically speaking, the implications of such transformations invite profound inquiry. The concept of the 'human norm' historically encapsulated a biologically anchored understanding of physical and mental capacities. This framework, however, is increasingly challenged by the emergence of enhancements that augment or transcend inherent capabilities. We are confronted with questions about the essence of humanity: Are humans defined solely by their biological heritage, or is there a fluidity that embraces technological integration as part of our evolutionary narrative?

This reflection becomes particularly pertinent in light of enhancements that stretch not only our physical attributes—such as strength, endurance, or resilience—but also our cognitive functions, emotional states, and sensory perceptions. As enhancements evolve, so too do the benchmarks of what is considered "normal." Society faces the prospect of a newly defined human experience, one where augmented individual capabilities become commonplace, leading us to contemplate whether those who choose to remain "unaltered" may be viewed as outdated or deficient. The very fabric of identity—intertwined with personal potential and societal expectations—may begin to shift, creating a chasm between those embracing enhancements and those who refrain.

Moreover, as we advance towards redefining human norms, the philosophical discourse expands to include ethical considerations. The evaluation of enhancements forces society to confront moral dilemmas regarding the intrinsic value of the natural human condition. Is it inherently good to seek improvement, or might we inadvertently undermine fundamental traits that form the bedrock of our humanity, such as empathy, vulnerability, and organic growth through experience? The quest for enhancement may yield physical and cognitive superiority, yet it also poses dangers of fostering elitism, devaluing traits attributed to the "non-enhanced," and questioning the authenticity of human connections.

The equation of human norms further extends to cultural and social implications. As augmented humans evolve, so will the social constructs that define relationships, responsibilities, and communal dynamics. These enhanced individuals might develop new modes of existence, creating communities formed around shared benefits and capabilities brought on by enhancement, potentially leading to a disconnect from traditional societal structures and values. This raises the pressing question: Can a cohesive social fabric exist amidst the disparity in enhancement levels, or does the proliferation of cybernetic modifications invite further fragmentation of society?

Yet alongside these challenges lie profound opportunities to cultivate an enriched understanding of humanity. With the ongoing blending of the biological and technological realms, we may discover insights into our existence that were previously obscured. The reevaluation of norms could usher in a more nuanced appreciation for individual differences, diverse capabilities, and the fluid nature of identity itself. Within this reimagined narrative, the definition of what it means to be human could be expanded to celebrate diversity in expression, intellect, and experience—encouraging a society that values both enhancement and the richness of unaltered humanity.

Navigating this evolving landscape involves us embracing a collective responsibility to shape the ethical frameworks guiding enhancements. As we redefine norms through technological evolution, the power of choice remains at the forefront. The dialogue surrounding what constitutes ethical enhancements—affirming the humanity within the enhancements—serves as a call to action, inviting individuals, communities, and policymakers to engage in conversations about the implications of these transformations, ensuring that humanity is not only augmented but also preserved amid shifting paradigms.

In summary, the endeavor to redefine the norms of humanity opens an expansive dialogue filled with philosophical, ethical, and cultural implications. As technology anchors itself deeper into the human experience, we are afforded an opportunity to not only challenge and redefine traditional concepts of identity and capability but also to foster a richer understanding of the human condition that embraces both enhancement and the irreplaceable essence of what it means to be human. Society's response to these transformations will encapsulate not only our aspirations but our commitment to navigating this remarkable evolution thoughtfully and ethically, setting the stage for a future where the redefined norms celebrate the expansive possibilities of the human experience.

5.2. The Ethical Dilemma of Access

The equitable access to and integration of technological advancements, particularly in the realm of cybernetic enhancements, presents a significant ethical dilemma. As we forge ahead into a future increasingly defined by the blending of biology and technology, the question of who has access to these transformative technologies looms large. The disparity in access to enhancements can exacerbate existing societal inequalities, leading to a potentially divided future where the enhanced and the unenhanced lead starkly different lives.

Throughout history, access to technology has often mirrored existing social stratifications—those with financial means, education, and resources are frequently the first to adopt innovative technologies. Cybernetic enhancements hold the potential to revolutionize personal capabilities, healthcare, and quality of life, yet without equitable access, they risk further entrenching the divide between socioeconomic classes. The advent of neural interfaces, advanced prosthetics, cognitive enhancements, and other transformative technologies could become markers of privilege, where the ability to significantly improve one's life hinges on wealth and access to advanced knowledge systems.

Consider the scenario where cognitive enhancement becomes commonplace. Individuals who can afford neural implants to augment memory and intelligence may excel in education and professional settings, ultimately translating enhanced cognitive abilities into economic advantages. Conversely, those without access to such enhancements could find themselves disadvantaged in increasingly competitive job markets. As cognitive capabilities become a determinant of success, this amplification of inequality could result in a society segmented along lines of enhancement—those who are enhanced may have access to better jobs, healthcare, and social mobility, while the unenhanced may face systemic barriers stalling their progress and potential.

Similarly, in the healthcare realm, access to genetic therapies, CRISPR technologies, and prosthetic developments will dictate health outcomes and quality of life. Those with less economic power may not be able to afford the necessary procedures to treat catastrophic injuries or genetic disorders, while wealthier individuals could employ genetic editing to eliminate hereditary diseases or enhance physical attributes. This divergence introduces ethical concerns, particularly around fairness and justice; it raises questions of who should be entitled to lifesaving technologies and who ultimately determines the value of human life when the ability to choose enhancements correlates so tightly with wealth.

Moreover, the implications of unequal access extend beyond the individual to broader societal dynamics. A populace divided by access to technology could lead to the emergence of a two-tiered society, fostering resentment, social unrest, and tension. The discourse around enhancement takes a darker turn as it becomes intertwined with issues of privilege—those left behind in this technological race may feel alienated or marginalized, thereby undermining societal cohesion. It also opens the door to conversely dangerous ideologies that may view the unenhanced as inferior, ultimately manifesting in discriminatory practices or policies that further entrench stigmas.

Addressing the ethical dilemma of access necessitates proactive measures on multiple fronts. Policymakers, ethicists, and technologists must come together to ensure that the ascent into a cybernetically enhanced age does not leave the vulnerable behind. Equitable access can be approached through frameworks that promote universal health coverage including provisions for new technologies, support for public research initiatives focused on reducing costs, and policies aimed at democratizing innovation to benefit broader swathes of society. A shift towards equitable access demands a commitment to fostering a future where all individuals can leverage technological advancements to improve their circumstances, thereby preventing the emergence of enhancement-based hierarchies.

Further, education systems must prioritize tech literacy, giving individuals from diverse backgrounds the skills and knowledge necessary to engage with emerging technologies. By providing equitable opportunities for education and technical training, society can empower individuals to become informed participants of their own evolutionary narrative, contributing to a more balanced and inclusive technological advancement.

Ultimately, the ethical dilemma of access to cybernetic enhancements underscores a crucial reality: our future will be shaped by the choices we make today. As we explore the expanding frontiers of technology, society must balance innovation with responsibility—actively working to ensure that advancements enrich lives across the spectrum rather than deepen existing divides. In doing so, we can aspire to a future characterized by inclusivity, empathy, and a shared commitment to harnessing technology to elevate the human experience for all.

5.3. Privacy in the Cybernetic Age

In the rapidly evolving landscape of the cybernetic age, privacy has emerged as a paramount concern. The integration of technology into daily life, fueled by a multitude of interconnected devices and platforms, has fundamentally transformed how we perceive and protect our personal data. As our lives become increasingly digitized, the potential risks associated with the collection, storage, and dissemination of personal information have escalated. This chapter explores these challenges, the implications for individual privacy, and potential solutions for safeguarding data in an era defined by technological advancement.

The interconnectedness of devices known as the Internet of Things (IoT) has revolutionized the way we live and interact with our environments. Smart home devices, wearables, and mobile applications track our habits, preferences, and even our health metrics in real time. While these innovations offer unparalleled convenience and insights, they also raise significant privacy concerns. The sheer volume of data generated and shared can expose individuals to potential misuse or unauthorized access. With countless systems collecting sensitive information, the risk of breaches, data leaks, and identity theft increases, prompting urgent discussions about who owns this data and how it should be protected.

As individuals navigate a world where their every digital interaction generates data, the notion of informed consent becomes particularly critical. Users often engage with terms of service that are lengthy and convoluted, leading to a limited understanding of how their data may be used, shared, or sold. The pervasive nature of data collection has normalized the relinquishing of privacy in exchange for services, thereby creating a dynamic where personal information is commodified. This commodification raises ethical questions about the extent to which individuals can genuinely control their data and the power dynamics at play between consumers and corporations.

Furthermore, the role of artificial intelligence in processing vast amounts of data introduces another layer of complexity. AI systems analyze user behavior to predict trends, tailor advertisements, and influence decision-making. While these algorithms can enhance user experience, they can also perpetuate biases, infringe on privacy, and lead to surveillance-like scenarios. The opacity of AI decision-making processes further complicates accountability, as users may remain unaware of how their data is being used or the implications of algorithmic determinations. This creates an urgent need for transparency in AI operations and a reassessment of the ethical standards that govern data utilization.

In addressing these risks, potential solutions for safeguarding personal data must prioritize both technology and policy. Developing robust security measures is essential for protecting data from breaches and unauthorized access. This includes implementing encryption, secure authentication protocols, and regular audits of data practices to ensure compliance with best practices for data protection. As technologies evolve, continual adaptation of security measures must be adopted to stay ahead of emerging vulnerabilities.

Additionally, fostering a culture of digital literacy is vital for empowering individuals to understand and manage their digital footprints. Educational initiatives should focus on elucidating concepts of privacy, data ownership, and informed consent. Programs that equip users with the knowledge to navigate their digital environments judiciously can encourage proactive decision-making regarding data sharing and enhance overall privacy awareness.

On a policy level, the enforcement of comprehensive data protection regulations is necessary to establish frameworks that prioritize user privacy. Legislation such as the General Data Protection Regulation (GDPR) in Europe sets a precedent for stringent data privacy laws that protect individual rights. Countries and organizations should consider implementing similar protective measures that enforce accountability on corporations, mandate transparency in data practices, and address data consumerism's ethical implications.

Tech companies have a critical role to play in prioritizing user privacy. By fostering ethical data practices, such as minimizing data collection to what is essential and offering users clear choices about data sharing, these companies can regain user trust and promote privacy-centric models. Implementing privacy-by-design principles, where user privacy is embedded in every stage of product development, empowers individuals while enhancing the overall integrity of digital systems.

As we advance deeper into the cybernetic age, the conversation surrounding privacy must remain dynamic and responsive to emerging technologies. Vigilance about the implications of interconnected systems and the evolving nature of data collection is essential. It requires not only individual awareness of privacy risks but also collective advocacy for fair policies that guard against exploitation and promote a balanced relationship between technological advancement and personal autonomy.

In conclusion, privacy in the cybernetic age is fraught with complexities arising from the integration of technology into our daily lives. The interconnectedness of devices and platforms presents inherent risks that necessitate robust solutions, including security measures, advocacy for legislation, and a culture of digital literacy. While the potential benefits of technology are profound, ensuring that individual privacy is respected and protected must be a guiding principle as we navigate the challenges and opportunities of this new era. The pursuit of a future where technological integration enhances human experiences without compromising personal privacy is not only desirable—it is imperative for the dignity and autonomy of individuals in an increasingly digitized world.

5.4. Cybernetic Enhancements and Identity

The integration of technological enhancements into our lives inevitably influences our sense of self and identity, challenging long-held notions of what it means to be human. As individuals contribute to and adopt advancements in cybernetic enhancements, the interplay between technology and personal identity evolves in ways that provoke both excitement and unease. The discussion of identity in this context involves several interrelated aspects, including the transformation of personal and social identity, the redefinition of authenticity, and the intersections of self-perception within a technologically augmented environment.

Fundamentally, the integration of technologies into our bodies and lives raises questions about the nature of self-identity. If a significant part of our cognitive or physical capabilities is enhanced or even replaced by machines, how do we define ourselves? Traditional ideas of identity based on biological or psychological continuity face significant challenges when technologies such as artificial limbs, neural implants, or genetic modifications become extensions of self. The concept of identity becomes fluid, stretching to encompass these enhancements while simultaneously prompting individuals to reconsider their relationship with their own physicality and cognition. For example, a person who relies on a bionic arm for functionality may begin to identify as an amalgamation of biological and artificial—a "cyborg"—effectively reshaping their narrative and personal identity.

Moreover, the adoption of technological enhancements can lead to a shift in social identity. As certain enhancements become markers of status or success, individuals may feel compelled to pursue augmentation to align with societal expectations. This phenomenon can create a societal divide between those who embrace enhancements and those who choose to remain unaltered. By emphasizing traits associated with enhancement, society sets new standards for achievement, potentially marginalizing individuals who choose not to augment themselves. The pressure to conform to an enhanced identity could lead to the perception that being unenhanced signifies inadequacy, further complicating the landscape of social identity.

This shift also prompts existential questions about authenticity. If identity is contingent upon the integration of technological advancements, how can authenticity be determined? Authenticity—the degree to which one believes their identity is genuine or true—may come under scrutiny as individuals grapple with the idea that their thoughts, emotions, or capabilities could be artificially enhanced or altered. The authenticity of experiences becomes intertwined with the nature of enhancement itself. For instance, if emotional states can be regulated through neuro-stimulation or cognitive functions amplified via artificial intelligence, how does this affect the essence of those experiences? This blending of the natural and artificial complicates not only self-perception but also interpersonal relationships, as the lines between genuine interactions and technologically mediated emotional exchanges blur.

Additionally, many individuals find themselves navigating the duality of embracing technology while grappling with inherent fears associated with losing their humanity. The narratives surrounding transhumanism often evoke a dichotomy between enhancement and the "natural" human experience, creating an internal struggle between progress and authenticity. As one contemplates the possibilities that cybernetic enhancements promise, the underlying fear of becoming less human, or alienating oneself from those who do not share similar enhancements, lingers in the background. This tension serves as a backdrop against which individuals must navigate their journeys of adopting and adapting to new identities in an increasingly augmented society.

Importantly, technology not only changes personal identity on an individual level but also influences collective identities. As people increasingly identify within communities focused on specific enhancements, a new social dynamic arises. Cyborg communities, for instance, celebrate the fusion of technology and humanity while fostering environments that promote understanding and acceptance of augmented identities. This sense of belonging within the context of shared experiences amongst the enhanced can create empowering narratives that challenge societal interpretations of identity. These communities not only encourage acceptance but often push for advocacy regarding rights and access to enhancements, defining a new stage in the conversation around identity and technology.

In addition to social and personal identity, the implications of adopting cybernetic enhancements uncover profound philosophical questions concerning the nature of consciousness and self-awareness. Enhancement technologies that modify cognitive processes challenge our understanding of consciousness as well. If enhancements enable individuals to gain insights, capabilities, or forms of intelligence beyond their natural limits, we are compelled to consider whether alterations to thought processes influence our self-awareness or the way we experience existence. The transformation of how we perceive ourselves, as both subjects and objects in a rapidly changing technological landscape, is a reminder of the profound implications enhancements can carry about the very fabric of our identities.

As we consider the relationship between technological enhancements and identity, it becomes increasingly clear that the influence of technology is not merely additive; it alters the qualitative experience of being human. Navigating these transformations requires continued engagement with complex ethical, philosophical, and psychological dimensions, emphasizing the need for informed dialogue surrounding these phenomena. Each individual's journey through enhancement will vary, ultimately contributing to an evolving collective narrative surrounding identity and technology—one that encompasses both the possibilities and the pitfalls of a cybernetic future. Thus, as we embrace the allure of enhancement, the ongoing exploration of identity in the age of technology will remain deeply relevant, guiding our understanding of ourselves as we enter this exciting yet daunting new frontier of human experience.

6. A New Frontier in Medicine

6.1. Eradicating Disease with Precision

In the ever-evolving landscape of healthcare, cybernetic advancements hold great promise in revolutionizing the diagnosis, treatment, and ultimately, the eradication of diseases. The traditional models of medicine, often reactive and generalized in approach, are being replaced with precise and personalized strategies fueled by innovative technologies. This shift towards precision medicine represents a fundamental rethinking of how we interact with health and disease, promoting an era where interventions are meticulously tailored to the unique biological makeup of the individual.

At the core of this transformation is the groundbreaking application of genomics—the study of an individual's DNA. Recent advancements in sequencing technologies have significantly decreased the costs and time associated with comprehensive genomic profiling, enabling healthcare practitioners to dissect the genetic underpinnings of diseases with unprecedented accuracy. By understanding the specific mutations and variations that contribute to an individual's health status, physicians can devise precise treatment plans that target the root causes of illnesses rather than their symptoms.

For instance, cancer treatment has historically relied on generalized protocols, but the advent of genomic sequencing allows for the identification of specific genetic mutations present in a tumor. This information empowers oncologists to select therapies that are more likely to be effective based on the tumor's unique genetic makeup, a practice known as targeted therapy. Drugs such as targeted molecular therapies and immunotherapies are now designed to interact with specific molecules on cancer cells, effectively shutting down their ability to grow and proliferate. This revolutionary approach not only enhances treatment efficacy but also minimizes the side effects often associated with conventional therapies like chemotherapy.

Additionally, the potential of CRISPR technology—the revolutionary gene-editing tool—is breaking down biological barriers and redefining disease eradication at its source. CRISPR enables precise alterations to an organism's DNA, which holds tremendous potential for correcting genetic defects and eliminating hereditary diseases before they manifest. In instances of conditions like sickle cell anemia or cystic fibrosis, targeted gene editing could potentially cure these disorders by correcting the specific mutations responsible for their symptoms directly within the patient's genome. Ongoing clinical trials are already testing CRISPR applications for a range of genetic disorders, creating a beacon of hope for individuals and families impacted by hereditary conditions.

As cybernetic enhancements coalesce with developments in artificial intelligence, the synergy creates new dimensions for disease management. Machine learning algorithms can analyze vast datasets generated through medical records, genetic profiles, and treatment outcomes to identify patterns that humans might overlook. These insights lead to predictive healthcare models that can forecast disease risk based on an individual's genetic predispositions and lifestyle factors, effectively allowing preventive measures to be implemented before disease onset.

Wearable technologies, embedded with sensors that continuously monitor vital signs and physiological parameters, further enhance this precision approach. Imagine a future where smart devices track blood glucose levels, heart rates, and even hormonal fluctuations in real-time, alerting individuals and their healthcare providers to early warning signs of health issues. Such proactive monitoring allows for timely intervention, reducing the probability of complications arising from chronic conditions. For instance, diabetes management could be revolutionized by smart insulin delivery systems that automatically adjust dosages based on real-time glucose levels, ensuring optimal control and minimizing health risks.

Furthermore, the field of personalized medicine extends beyond genetics to encompass lifestyle factors such as diet, exercise, and environment. The integration of data from various sources—including genomics, wearables, and electronic health records—fuels a holistic understanding of health that empowers individuals to make informed choices. Nutrition plans can be tailored to an individual's genetic predispositions, optimizing dietary interventions by focusing on the nutrients required to combat specific health risks. This transcendence from a one-size-fits-all approach to a highly personalized one sharpens the preventive capabilities of modern healthcare.

Nevertheless, the advancement of precision medicine and the eradication of diseases also raise ethical and societal questions that must be carefully navigated. Considerations regarding access to these technologies emerge as critical; as cutting-edge treatment methods become available, disparities in healthcare access could widen, especially for marginalized communities. The democratization of precision medicine, ensuring equitable access for all individuals regardless of socioeconomic status, is imperative to avoid creating a world where only the affluent can afford potentially life-saving interventions.

Moreover, we must address the philosophical implications of editing our genetic makeup. As society grapples with the idea of manipulating genes, discussions regarding consent, autonomy, and the potential long-term effects of such alterations are essential. Ethical frameworks will need to evolve alongside technological innovations to ensure responsible practices are implemented, safeguarding not just individual rights but also the integrity of human biology as a whole.

In summary, the era of cybernetic advancements is ushering in a new frontier in medicine, promising to transform our understanding of disease management and eradication with unprecedented precision. By harnessing the power of genomic insights, artificial intelligence, and wearable technology, we stand on the brink of healthcare revolution—one where interventions are personalized, proactive, and, ultimately, more effective. As we navigate the complexities surrounding these innovations, striking a balance between technological possibilities and ethical considerations will be paramount in realizing a future where diseases can be meticulously targeted and eradicated, guiding humanity towards a healthier existence.

6.2. Enhancements for Rehabilitation

The field of rehabilitation has been profoundly transformed by technological innovations, which have significantly enhanced the recovery process and improved the quality of life for individuals coping with disabilities or injuries. As we delve into the transformative power of these advancements, we can explore various dimensions of rehabilitation, ranging from the design and implementation of advanced prosthetics to the integration of computer-assisted therapy and neurotechnologies that facilitate motor and cognitive recovery.

One of the most striking advancements in rehabilitation is the development of advanced prosthetics. Modern prosthetic devices increasingly incorporate robotics and smart technologies that work in tandem with users' natural biological systems. Unlike traditional prosthetics, which often had limited functionality and were intentionally designed to mimic lost limbs, contemporary devices actively interpret signals from the user's musculature or nervous system, providing intuitive movement and responsiveness. For example, myoelectric prosthetics utilize electromyography (EMG) sensors to detect muscle contractions, allowing users to control the movement of the limb naturally. This innovation affords individuals greater autonomy and a sense of normalcy, enabling them to perform everyday tasks with improved proficiency and less effort.

Robotics not only enhances limb functionality but also redefines rehabilitation practices for individuals requiring therapy post-injury. Robotic exoskeletons, designed to aid in the recovery of motor function, can assist patients with mobility challenges, including spinal cord injuries or strokes. These devices support the user's weight while providing powered assistance to enable walking. Physical therapists can utilize exoskeletons to guide patients through repetitive motions, restoring strength and coordination over time. The adaptability of robotic systems allows for tailored rehabilitation programs, actively accommodating individual needs and advancing patient care.

In parallel, computer-assisted therapy is gaining traction as an effective method for facilitating neurorehabilitation. Virtual reality (VR) and augmented reality (AR) technologies create immersive environments to simulate real-world experiences, promoting engagement in rehabilitation exercises. For example, a stroke survivor might engage with VR too, requiring them to grasp virtual objects, enhancing their motor skills through a playful yet scientifically grounded approach. These immersive therapies not only aid in physical recovery but also stimulate cognitive processes, fostering neural plasticity—the brain's ability to reorganize itself by forming new neural connections in response to learning and experience. This is particularly crucial for individuals recovering from traumatic brain injuries or strokes, as cognitive rehabilitation becomes integral to their journey back to independence.

Additionally, telehealth and digital health applications are revolutionizing the accessibility and reach of rehabilitation services. By leveraging remote monitoring technologies, healthcare providers can track patients' progress in real-time, providing feedback and interventions wherever the patient may be. Smart devices equipped with sensors can collect data on movement patterns, gait analysis, and overall activity levels, offering valuable insights for clinicians to adjust rehabilitation plans accordingly. This approach not only enhances patient accountability but also fosters a sense of connectedness, as individuals feel supported by their care teams despite physical distances.

Assistive technologies are also playing a vital role in creating more inclusive environments for individuals with disabilities. From communication devices that empower individuals with speech deficits to mobility aids that enhance navigation for those with vision impairments, these tools facilitate independence and social participation. For instance, eye-tracking technology enables individuals with mobility impairments to interact with digital interfaces using only their eye movements, opening avenues for engagement in work, education, and social interactions that would otherwise be challenging.

Moreover, the integration of artificial intelligence within rehabilitation technology serves to personalize recovery plans. Machine learning algorithms can analyze vast data sets to develop individualized exercise regimens based on patients' unique needs, preferences, and response to treatment. AI-driven applications can provide real-time feedback on patients' performance, allowing them to adjust their efforts and enhancing motivation through gamification strategies, rewarding progress, and facilitating a sense of achievement.

While technological advancements in rehabilitation offer tremendous potential, they also prompt crucial ethical and accessibility discussions. As we push the boundaries of innovation, it is vital to consider the implications of a technology-driven rehabilitation landscape. Access to high-quality rehabilitation technologies—and the training necessary to utilize them—must be equitable, ensuring that all individuals, regardless of socioeconomic status, can benefit from advances that improve their quality of life. The potential for disparities in access to these transformative tools could exacerbate existing inequalities, making it imperative for healthcare systems to adopt policies that prioritize comprehensive access and affordability.

In conclusion, the innovations in rehabilitation technologies signify a remarkable shift in how we approach recovery and quality of life for individuals with disabilities or injuries. From advanced prosthetics and robotic exoskeletons to virtual reality therapy and AI-driven personalized treatment plans, each advancement contributes to an increasingly holistic and empowering rehabilitation experience. As we continue to explore these technologies, it is essential to balance innovation with ethical considerations, striving for a future where all individuals can access and benefit from the transformative power of cybernetic enhancements in rehabilitation. The journey toward better recovery and quality of life is not solely defined by technology, but by our commitment to inclusivity and the dignity of all individuals in the pursuit of well-being.

6.3. Genetic Engineering and Longevity

Genetic engineering stands at the cutting edge of modern science, championing the endeavor to not only understand the human genome but to actively manipulate it, with the ultimate goal of enhancing longevity and resilience against diseases. As we delve into the intricacies of this profound field, we observe how scientific breakthroughs in genetic research and biotechnological innovations promise to extend life expectancy and elevate the quality of human existence. The implications of these advancements are vast, extending into ethical debates, societal considerations, and personal health experiences.

The notion of extending human life is not a contemporary concept; it has been a longstanding aspiration of humanity, mirrored in literature, philosophy, and the collective imagination across cultures. The quest for immortality or at least a significant extension of life has permeated human history, suggesting a deep-rooted desire to overcome mortality. Today, advancements in genetic engineering offer tangible pathways towards this age-old pursuit.

Central to this transformation are our increasing capabilities in gene editing, primarily through tools like CRISPR-Cas9. This groundbreaking technology allows scientists to edit specific DNA sequences, enabling precise alterations to genes responsible for hereditary diseases, allowing not only for the treatment of genetic disorders but also unearthing potential enhancements to human resilience. For instance, research suggests that targeting the genes involved in cellular senescence—cells that lose their ability to divide and contribute to aging—could lead to greater vitality. By reprogramming these cellular pathways, we could, theoretically, slow down the aging process itself, heralding a future where individuals may live longer, healthier lives.

Moreover, advancements in genetic engineering allow for the exploration of resilience-enhancing traits. Studies are underway to examine the genes that govern aging and resilience in certain species notorious for their long lifespans, such as the naked mole rat and certain species of tortoises. By identifying and understanding the unique genetic characteristics that confer longevity in these animals, researchers aim to translate this knowledge to humans. This could lead to potential interventions focused on gene therapy, where identified longevity genes are integrated or activated in human DNA to enhance our innate biological resilience against age-related diseases, cancer, cardiovascular issues, and neurodegenerative conditions.

Additionally, the implications of genetic engineering for modifying human traits to encourage longevity involve intricate ethical discussions. The question of eugenics—essentially the idea of improving the genetic quality of a population—re-emerges in contemporary discourse, now transformed into a discussion around enhancements and designer traits. As capabilities expand to include the potential editing of genes to confer resistance against degenerative diseases or age-related conditions, society must grapple with the moral implications of choosing which traits to enhance or diminish. The potential for creating a genetically modified "elite" human population raises fundamental questions about social equity, individual autonomy, and the ethical boundaries of altering human genetics.

Further, the role of epigenetics—the study of changes in gene expression that do not involve alterations to the underlying DNA sequence—plays a fundamental part in longevity research as well. Environmental impacts, lifestyle choices, and behavior can modify epigenetic markers, influencing an individual's health outcomes. By understanding how external factors interact with gene expression, we gain insights into how certain habits and environments can promote longevity. This multidimensional approach allows for an integration of genetics with lifestyle interventions—a strategy that promotes a holistic view on health and longevity, advocating individualized plans that incorporate not just genetic modification but also proper nutrition, exercise, and mental well-being.

As we embrace the potential of genetic engineering to extend lifespan, new considerations emerge regarding the nature of aging and its societal implications. Longevity has historically been tied to the concepts of wisdom and experience; as people live longer, the paradigms surrounding work, retirement, and intergenerational relationships may shift dramatically. Longer lifespans could lead to re-examining societal structures, necessitating adjustments in healthcare provision, pension systems, and community support networks. The potential for age-related societal reorganization compels society to reconsider how we value age, capacity, and the roles of older adults as contributors to the fabric of society.

Maintaining health throughout extended lifespans is paramount, and the risks associated with genetic interventions, while promising, also call for vigilant oversight and rigorous research. A multifaceted approach that embraces a fusion of technological healing, active lifestyle, psychological resilience, and community support stands as our best chance for not only living longer but enjoying a higher quality of life during those years.

Predictably, the ongoing advancements in genetic engineering and its implications for longevity provoke profound dialogues about what it means to be human in an age characterized by unprecedented biotechnology. As we venture into this transformative era, we must reflect on the ethical landscapes we navigate, ensuring that the promises of longevity are equitably shared across diverse populations. The urgent exploration of genetic engineering and its connection to extending life illuminates not only the excitement of biomedical innovation but also the essential pursuit of a good life—one rooted in health, dignity, and meaningful connections with others.

As we stand on the threshold of what might be considered a genetic renaissance in healthcare, the confluence of technological innovation and ethical embodiment will determine how we harness these advancements for humanity's benefit, marking a pivotal evolution in our understanding of life, health, and longevity.

6.4. The Future of Personalized Medicine

The exploration of personalized medicine represents an intersection of cutting-edge technology and individualized care, where therapeutic approaches are increasingly tailored to the distinct genetic and biomolecular characteristics of each patient. This revolutionary paradigm shift signifies an essential departure from traditional "one-size-fits-all" medical practices, providing a more nuanced approach that acknowledges the variability inherent in human biology. As advancements in data collection and analysis evolve, personalized medicine is paving pathways toward more effective, precise, and patient-centric healthcare, necessitating a consideration of its implications for medical practice, ethics, and society.

Central to the future of personalized medicine is the ability to leverage individual genetic profiles to guide medical interventions. The completion of the Human Genome Project provided an unprecedented depth of insight into human genetics, mapping the approximately 20,000 genes in human DNA. Today, genomics technology has advanced to the point where comprehensive genomic sequencing is not only more accessible and affordable but also actionable. Clinicians can analyze an individual's genetic information, identifying specific mutations, susceptibilities to diseases, and responses to various treatments. This detailed understanding can significantly enhance decision-making processes, allowing healthcare professionals to select therapies tailored to an individual's genetic makeup and likely responses.

For instance, in the realm of oncology, advancements in personalized medicine have led to the rise of targeted therapies that focus on the unique genetic mutations present within a patient's cancer. By identifying specific alterations in tumor DNA, oncologists can deploy treatments designed to inhibit the growth of cancer cells more effectively, minimizing side effects and increasing treatment efficacy. This method not only exemplifies the concept of personalized medicine but also signifies a greater recognition of the complexity of disease interactions, moving beyond broad treatment protocols toward precision interventions.

Furthermore, pharmacogenomics—the study of how genes affect an individual's response to medications—offers exciting possibilities for optimizing drug therapies. By determining a patient's genetic profile, healthcare providers can predict how they might metabolize or react to certain medications, subsequently guiding the selection and dosage of drugs. This reduces the trial-and-error approach often associated with prescribing medications, ensuring that individuals receive the most suitable therapy from the outset. Consequently, the move toward personalized medicine could significantly improve medication adherence and outcomes while minimizing adverse effects and the likelihood of complications.

As we delve deeper into the future of personalized medicine, the integration of artificial intelligence (AI) and machine learning stands out as a transformative trend. With the potential to analyze vast datasets quickly, these technologies can uncover patterns and insights that aid in developing predictive models for disease risk and treatment responses. For instance, AI algorithms can sift through genomic data, electronic health records, and clinical findings to establish correlations that inform clinical decision-making. This approach enriches personalized medicine by providing clinicians with tools to mitigate risks and improve intervention strategies, moving toward a proactive model of healthcare.

While the promise of personalized medicine is compelling, it raises significant ethical questions that demand careful scrutiny. The complexity of patient data, particularly genetic information, necessitates stringent considerations around privacy, consent, and data ownership. Safeguarding sensitive information becomes paramount as the potential for data breaches presents significant risks to individuals' privacy and autonomy. Establishing robust policies regarding data management and protective measures is essential to maintain trust in personalized medicine.

Moreover, as personalized medicine continues to proliferate, ensuring equitable access to these groundbreaking interventions is paramount. The potential for disparities to arise based on socio-economic factors poses ethical dilemmas regarding who benefits from advancements in healthcare. If access to personalized therapies remains limited to affluent individuals, a wider gap in health outcomes could emerge, exacerbating existing healthcare inequalities. The pursuit of an inclusive healthcare system that guarantees equal access to personalized medicine across diverse populations must remain a fundamental tenet of this evolution.

Additionally, the notion of "designer" enhancements, where genetic modifications occur not only to treat illnesses but also for the purpose of augmenting human capabilities, presents fresh ethical complexities. This conversation echoes broader debates on genetic engineering and the implications of manipulating the human genome. Should society embrace modifications that enhance intelligence, physical abilities, or other traits, and under what circumstances? Addressing these profound ethical considerations will require robust public discourse, collaborative policymaking, and thorough examination of the aspirations and responsibilities tied to personalized medicine.

As we venture into the future of personalized medicine, the interplay between technology, ethics, and patient care will shape a transformative healthcare landscape. The potential to tailor treatments based on genetic profiles heralds the arrival of a new era in medicine, one that prioritizes individualization and precision while continuing to grapple with the responsibilities accompanying such tremendous advancements. By fostering an inclusive dialogue around personalization in care and embracing the ethical dimensions that arise, society can harness the vast potential of personalized medicine to cultivate healthier, more resilient individuals and communities in the years to come. The journey toward understanding ourselves at a molecular level holds the promise of a future where medicine is not just reactive but transformative, leading us not only to longer lives but also to lives enriched with health, dignity, and purpose.

7. Beyond Human: The Posthuman Perspective

7.1. Envisioning the Posthuman Condition

In the exploration of the posthuman condition, we stand on the precipice of dramatically redefined concepts of existence, identity, and community. Technology is no longer merely an extension of our capabilities; it has become a core component of human evolution, prompting us to rethink what it means to be human. This transformation offers an opportunity to envision a future where the line between biological and technological life becomes increasingly blurred, leading us toward the possibility of a posthuman existence.

To fathom this evolution, one must consider the trajectory of technological advancement that has historically redefined humanity. Early humans harnessed tools to survive. As advancements proliferated —from the wheel to the computer—each transformation not only augmented human capability but reshaped our relationships with our environments and with one another. We now find ourselves at a crucial juncture where technologies like AI, genetic engineering, and neurotechnology promise not just enhancements of our traits but a profound rethinking of identity and existence itself.

The posthuman condition invites speculation about a new species altogether—a being that transcends the limitations of flesh, extending physical and cognitive capabilities through augmentation. Imagine a future where neurotechnology allows us to enhance memory and cognition at will or where bioengineered modifications enable humans to thrive in diverse environments, from the depths of the ocean to the surface of other planets. In this scenario, humanity would not merely adapt to technology; it would coexist symbiotically with it, resulting in a shared evolution.

Within this framework, the notion of individuality is poised to undergo a fundamental transformation. As we integrate technologies capable of recording, sharing, and enhancing human thought and experience, our identities may become more communal and interconnected. The prospect of collective consciousness—where individuals contribute to a shared cognitive landscape—challenges traditional ideas of personal identity. Rather than seeing ourselves as isolated entities, we may begin to define our identities through our connections to others, facilitated by technological mediation.

The implications of enhanced connectivity extend to our understanding of empathy, communication, and collaboration. The future could hold scenarios where minds link seamlessly through advanced networks, sharing experiences, thoughts, and emotions instantaneously. This hive consciousness presents a potential shift in social dynamics, where the collective wellbeing surpasses individual desires and priorities. Societal challenges could be addressed collaboratively, fostering a deeper understanding of diverse perspectives and experiences.

However, envisioning the posthuman condition does not come without its ethical conundrums. The potential consequences of merging minds raise questions about consent, autonomy, and individuality. If our thoughts and experiences can be shared instantaneously, what becomes of personal privacy? The blending of consciousness may blur the distinctions between self and other, leading to philosophical questions about ownership—who is accountable for thoughts and actions in a shared cognitive space? Exploring these questions is essential in delineating the contours of posthuman ethics.

As we delve into the implications of overcoming natural death through biotechnologies, the posthuman condition forces a reevaluation of mortality. The notion of biotechnological interventions extending life indefinitely evokes strong ethical considerations—would a society that enables immortality carry the weight of overpopulation, resource scarcity, and diminished meaning in life? The quest to surpass biological limits invites debates surrounding the natural cycle of life and the virtues of aging. What would it mean for our understanding of self-worth, legacy, and the human experience if death were no longer an inevitable conclusion?

The artistic expressions of the cybernetic future play a vital role in shaping the narrative surrounding the posthuman condition. Creative minds across various disciplines—literature, visual arts, music, and performance—reflect and critique the enhancement narrative, often offering poignant insights into the emotional, social, and ethical ramifications of our technologically driven destiny. Artistic explorations provide a platform for questioning and imagining the implications of what it means to be human in this brave new world.

As we stand at the threshold of this transformative age, the exploration of the posthuman condition invites us to engage thoughtfully with the possibilities before us. The future teems with potential to redefine existence as we know it, challenging us to envision a life interwoven with technology while grappling with the ethics and philosophies that arise alongside such advancements. In this exciting yet uncertain landscape, we have the opportunity to sculpt an inclusive, empathetic, and dynamic vision of life that honors both our biological roots and our aspirations for a transcendent future. The journey into the posthuman condition implores us to reflect on our shared humanity and collaboratively shape a future that realizes the vast potential of the human experience in harmony with technology.

7.2. Merging Minds: Hive Consciousness

In the exploration of hive consciousness, we find ourselves at the intersection of technology, identity, and community, where the merging of minds transcends traditional notions of individuality. This concept, while seemingly utopian, serves as a canvas for envisioning a future where collective intelligence manifests through interconnectedness, cooperation, and shared experiences. The dynamics of hive consciousness invite us to reflect on the implications of thought-sharing technologies, cognitive merging, and the transformation of human interaction in a cybernetic age.

At the heart of hive consciousness lies the potential for a new form of communication—one that transcends the spoken word and enters the realm of direct thought exchange. Imagine a future where advanced neural interfaces or brain-computer interfaces (BCIs) enable individuals to connect with one another at a cognitive level. Instead of relying solely on verbal communication, thoughts, emotions, and sensory experiences could be transmitted instantaneously, creating a profound sense of unity and empathy among participants. In such a reality, traditional language barriers may dissipate, giving way to a deeper understanding of one another's experiences and perspectives.

The concept of hive consciousness challenges the prevailing paradigms of individualism that have shaped human interaction for centuries. Instead of a society where success is often measured by personal achievement or competition, a hive mentality promotes a harmonious coexistence in which shared goals and cooperative processes take precedence. This shift could redefine social structures —fostering communities that prioritize collective well-being over individual pursuits. The emergence of such communities would encourage collaboration toward common goals, whether addressing societal challenges, environmental issues, or advancing knowledge.

However, while the promise of hive consciousness is alluring, it raises profound ethical dilemmas related to autonomy, consent, and the very nature of identity. As individuals become more interconnected through thought-sharing technologies, questions about personal agency and identity will inevitably surface. Could the distinctions that define us as individuals begin to blur? Would the essence of the self be lost in the amalgamation of thoughts and experiences, or would it transform into a new form of communal identity that includes a rich tapestry of voices?

The ethical implications of enabling hive consciousness extend far beyond philosophical inquiries; they necessitate careful consideration of the power dynamics involved in such connectivity. Who controls the shared consciousness? Would individuals be able to opt-out of engagement, or would societal pressures compel everyone to participate? The potential risks associated with manipulating collective intelligence demand robust ethical frameworks to ensure that the merging of minds enhances human experience without infringing upon individual rights or freedoms.

Furthermore, the implications of hive consciousness for creativity and innovation are of particular interest. Traditional models of creativity often celebrate individual genius; however, in a collective cognitive environment, innovation could emerge from the synergy of multiple minds collaborating in real-time. New ideas could proliferate exponentially, informed by the diverse insights and perspectives of a connected populace. This collaborative creativity might give rise to groundbreaking solutions to challenges that seem insurmountable today, as the collective intellect converges on complex problems from a multitude of angles.

Yet, the pursuit of hive consciousness invites us to evaluate the depth and quality of connections formed through technology. While the ability to share thoughts seamlessly offers immense potential for empathy and understanding, the richness of human relationships often thrives on the nuance of exclusive, personal interactions. Would the ability to connect with countless individuals dilute the intimacy that characterizes close relationships? How do we mitigate the risks of oversimplified connections or superficial interactions in a world where thought-sharing becomes ubiquitous?

As we contemplate the future of hive consciousness, we are confronted with the need for frameworks that guard against the exploitation of collective intelligence. The potential for using cognitive networks to manipulate opinions, spread disinformation, or foster echo chambers poses a grave ethical challenge. Maintaining integrity and authenticity in a world where thoughts can be transmitted and influenced instantaneously becomes paramount. As stewards of this emerging domain, it will be essential to champion responsible technological usage and foster awareness of the ethical implications tied to the merging of minds.

In conclusion, the vision of hive consciousness presents a transformative possibility for humanity, where the merging of minds offers a new frontier for communication, collaboration, and collective understanding. As we navigate this uncharted territory, we must remain vigilant in addressing the ethical uncertainties that accompany such profound interconnectivity. The journey into hive consciousness invites introspection on our individual and collective identities, challenging us to harmonize the potential for enhanced humanity with the preservation of autonomy, authenticity, and ethical responsibility. Through thoughtful exploration and dialogue, we can aspire to create a future where hive consciousness enriches the human experience, promoting empathy, cooperation, and a deeper connection among all individuals.

7.3. Amendments to Mortality

In a world increasingly characterized by rapid technological advancements, the philosophical and ethical considerations surrounding human mortality have come to the forefront of public discourse. The potential to overcome natural death through biotechnology invites an intricate examination of what it entails to extend, enhance, and ultimately redefine the human condition. This chapter grapples with pivotal questions: What would it mean to eliminate aging and disease as natural phenomena? How might this alteration affect individual identity, societal values, and our understanding of life itself?

At the heart of this exploration lies the concept of longevity, whose implications reach far beyond medical outcomes. Historically, humanity has regarded death as an inevitable conclusion to life— a perspective woven into cultural narratives, religious beliefs, and existential philosophies. The emergence of biotechnologies capable of extending human life forms a challenge to this perspective, thrusting society into an ideological discourse about the nature of life, purpose, and the value of existence. The prospect of dramatically increasing life expectancy raises fundamental questions about the meaning and quality of life lived in such an extended state.

From a medical standpoint, interventions involving genetic engineering, stem cell therapy, and advanced regenerative technologies hold the promise of reversing the aging process, repairing cellular damage, and enhancing overall health. The potential for individuals to live longer, healthier lives appeals to universal desires for vitality, fulfillment, and sustained contributions to society. However, as we stand at the precipice of opportunities to fundamentally alter biology and defeat death, ethical dilemmas emerge that challenge our conceptual foundations.

One of the most pressing ethical questions concerns the implications of extended lifespans for individual identity and agency. If individuals are granted the capacity to live indefinitely, the essence of what it means to grow old and confront mortality will be irrevocably altered. The traditional wisdom and experience associated with aging may lose significance if everyone retains their youth and vitality. Additionally, the prospect of infinite life raises questions about how people would choose to spend these extended years. Would individuals pursue meaningful goals, or would they become desensitized to time, risking a dilution of the urgency that often accompanies human experience?

The societal ramifications of overcoming natural death extend into the realm of resource allocation and intergenerational dynamics. An aging population living for centuries could place immense strain on financial, environmental, and social systems. Questions arise: If longevity is feasible, who gets to access it? Will socio-economic inequalities deepen as affluent individuals extend their lives while marginalized groups lack access to life-enhancing technologies? Moreover, as people live longer, traditional notions of family structures and community interrelations may shift. The relationships between generations could transform, creating complex dynamics around caregiving, support systems, and inheritance.

Further complicating the dialogue is the potential of technological integration to alter our relationship with death itself. The idea of "conquering" mortality introduces ethical discussions surrounding the appropriate approaches to life, death, and identity. Is it ethical to pursue the elimination of death when it has been an inherent part of the human experience? Societies may grapple with existential inquiries about the value of life if the concept of death becomes more abstract, leading to philosophical tensions when humans confront their mortality within technological contexts.

Moreover, the emergence of potential disparities in access to life-extending technologies emphasizes the necessity for robust ethical frameworks. The anticipation of a divided society—including both enhanced and unenhanced individuals—poses challenges to notions of equity and social justice. Governments, ethics boards, and researchers must collaboratively engage in conversations to establish policies that safeguard against exploitation, ensuring that access to life-preserving treatments is available to all, regardless of their socioeconomic standing.

Engagement with the public discourse surrounding the amendments to mortality necessitates not only scientific exploration but also a wider cultural dialogue that articulates the diverse perspectives and lived experiences of individuals regarding life, death, and the nature of existence. Artists, philosophers, and storytellers are crucial in shaping how society perceives these advancements, incorporating ethics, culture, and existential considerations into conversations about enhanced longevity. They offer reflections that remind us of the human experience's complexity, ultimately guiding us toward nuanced understandings of what life and death mean in an era marked by biotechnological innovations.

As we explore the ethical considerations surrounding the possibilities of overcoming natural death through biotechnologies, it becomes clear that the journey toward enhanced longevity is not merely about extending life itself—it is a profound inquiry into how we define life, agency, identity, and humanity in a rapidly evolving landscape. Acknowledging these discussions prepares us not only to navigate the advancements of the future but also to reflect on the core values that will guide our evolving relationship with life and mortality in an increasingly artificial world. The amendments to mortality present us with opportunities and challenges that demand thoughtful engagement grounded in ethical stewardship and a commitment to the human experience.

7.4. Artistic Expressions of Cybernetic Culture

Artistic expressions in the context of cybernetic culture serve as a vital lens through which society can explore and critique the implications of technological advancements on humanity. As the boundaries between human and machine blur, artists find themselves at the forefront of shaping narratives that invite contemplation, provoke debate, and elucidate the emotional and ethical complexities of living in a cyber-enhanced world. From visual art to literature and performance, creators are harnessing their creative powers to navigate the challenges and possibilities heralded by the rise of cybernetics, leading to a rich tapestry of cultural expressions that speak to our collective anxieties, hopes, and curiosities about the future.

Visual artists have taken bold approaches to depict the nuances of human-technology integration. One prominent trend is the infusion of elements of technology into traditional artistic mediums, where artists manipulate tools like 3D printing, virtual reality, and augmented reality to craft immersive experiences that resonate with audiences. For example, installations that utilize augmented reality allow viewers to interact with digital representations of themselves or their environments, effectively demonstrating the fluidity of identity in a cybernetic age. Artists like Rafael Lozano-Hemmer create interactive pieces that underscore the surveillance state, investigating the implications of constant digital monitoring while encouraging viewers to reflect on their own connectivity and identity within the digital realm.

Similarly, the realm of digital art has flourished, giving rise to unique forms of expression that embody the ethos of cybernetic culture. The emergence of generative art—created through algorithms and computational systems—challenges preconceived notions of authorship and creativity. Artists like Casey Reas, co-creator of Processing, use computer code to generate nonlinear, evolving artworks, emphasizing collaboration between human intention and machine outputs. This approach invites introspection on the nature of creativity in a world where machines can produce works indistinguishable from those created by human hands. Through generative art, creators draw attention to the intersection between artist and machine, blurring traditional boundaries of artistic practice while reflecting on the dynamic relationship between creators and their technological tools.

Literature has also embraced the themes of cybernetic culture, gripping readers with stories that dissect the implications of enhancement technologies, artificial intelligence, and posthumanism. Authors such as William Gibson and Donna Haraway navigate complex narratives that scrutinize the entanglements of biology and technology. Gibson's seminal work "Neuromancer" is a foundational text in the genre of cyberpunk, depicting a future where human consciousness interfaces with cyberspace and artificial intelligences, challenging readers to confront the existential dilemmas of identity and reality in an increasingly digital landscape. Haraway's "A Cyborg Manifesto" offers a radical perspective, proposing the cyborg as a metaphor for hybrid identities that defy traditional binaries—an embodied reflection of the complexities of gender, race, and technology in a posthuman world.

Furthermore, performance art emerges as a visceral medium for exploring the tensions between embodied humanity and machine enhancements. Artists like Stelarc have famously experimented with their bodies, integrating technologies such as robotics and prosthetics to transcend biological limitations. Stelarc's performances, which often involve suspending his body from hooks or utilizing robotic limbs, provoke questions about the relationship between the self and technology. By actively merging bodily experiences with technological augmentation, performance artists invite audiences to confront their discomforts and fascinations about becoming cyborgs, forcing a re-examination of the perceived boundaries of the human body.

The exploration of cybernetic culture is also manifested in emerging forms like bioart, where artists utilize living organisms as their medium. Artists such as Eduardo Kac, who is renowned for his creation of the genetically modified glowing rabbit named Alba, challenge ethical considerations linked to bioengineering and genetic editing. Kac's work raises critical questions about the manipulation of life forms, inviting exploration of humanity's role as creators and the consequences of altering nature. Through bioart, creators provoke discourse surrounding responsibility and ethics in a world increasingly dominated by biotechnologies, emphasizing the necessity of balancing innovation with conscience.

In addressing the emotional landscape of cybernetics, artists create culturally resonant pieces that traverse themes of longing, alienation, and connection. The psychological impact of living in a hyperconnected world is poignantly reflected through numerous artistic expressions. Filmmakers, such as Spike Jonze with "Her," offer reflective narratives depicting the search for intimacy and connection in a world where human relationships are often replaced or mediated by artificial intelligences. Through stories like this, creators tap into the deep anxieties surrounding technology's encroachment on our emotional lives, highlighting the fragility of authentic connections amidst the allure of artificial fulfillment.

Artistic expressions of cybernetic culture ultimately serve as critical commentaries on the futures we are crafting. By challenging audiences to engage with the implications of technological integration into daily life, artists illuminate both the potential benefits and perils of cybernetic enhancements. They offer vital spaces for dialogue and reflection, encouraging a reassessment of our identities, relationships, and societal structures as we stand on the cusp of profound transformation.

As this narrative unfolds, the arts will continue to play an essential role in shaping perceptions and creating frameworks for understanding our evolving relationship with technology. In doing so, artistic expressions invite society to not only envision the possibilities of a cybernetic future but also consider the ethical responsibilities that accompany the journey toward enhancement. Through this multifaceted exploration, art remains pivotal in mirroring and questioning the essence of humanity in an age of machines, challenging us to ponder: what does it truly mean to be human in a world where the lines between man and machine are constantly shifting? The answers, inspired by artistic reflections, become increasingly relevant as we navigate the complexities of a cybernetically enhanced existence.